The New Multichannel, Integrated Marketing: 29 Trends for Creating a Multichannel, Integrated Campaign to Boost Your Profits Now

Craig A. Huey

Media Specialists

i

Foreword

Over the past few years, there have been multiple major trends in marketing that have made it possible for businesses to grow faster than ever.

One of the most exciting new trends that's impacting every business in America is the trend of multichannel, integrated marketing.

Never before have such powerful channels of marketing been available in such a focused, targeted and comprehensive way.

Multichannel integrated marketing is accountable, scientific and measurable – and the results are phenomenal.

Since it's such a new form of marketing, we wanted to put together as comprehensive of a directory and road-map to success as we could.

Feel free to contact me if you have any questions – (310) 212-5727.

Craig Huey, President

Creative Direct Marketing Group, Inc.

Nobody knows direct response and digital marketing better.

The New Multichannel, Integrated Marketing: 29 Trends for Creating a
Multichannel, Integrated Campaign to Boost Your Profits Now

To my smart and beautiful wife Shelly, whose insights keep me on track. She has been my gift from God, best friend, cheerleader and prayer warrior.

To my clients, who have trusted me with their marketing, advertising, growth and expansion. I am honored and eternally grateful to them.

A special thanks to members of my team for making this book become a reality.

Caleb Huey; an expert of the benefits of multichannel marketing who has joined me in panels, seminars, webinars, speeches and in private meetings. What Caleb brings to the table is true transformational wisdom that launches successful campaigns.

Kelsey Yarnell; an avid copywriter who has done the research and clarified and crafted a complex issue into readable, dynamic content. Without her skills and wisdom, this book would not have happened.

Kent Barry; an editor whose wisdom and insights make everything more understandable.

Finally, I thank God for directing my path, not just for my career but for my entire life. It is in Him whom I place my trust. (Proverbs 3:5,6) I can do all this through Him who gives me strength. (Philippians 4:13)

Table of Contents

PART FOUR

PART FIVE

Part One

Introduction to Multichannel, Integrated Marketing

In Chapters 1–3, you'll get an overview of multichannel, integrated marketing ... and discover why this revolutionary approach to marketing could transform your business.

You'll also learn how to use high-level strategies to target your "perfect prospects" ... and get maximum response to your multichannel, integrated marketing.

CHAPTER 1

The New Multichannel, Integrated Marketing and Advertising

Entrepreneurs and company presidents are often confused ... even overwhelmed ... with choosing the most cost-effective and powerful ways to:

- Generate leads and convert them to sales
- Bring in new customers faster and more efficiently
- Dominate their market with an exciting product or service
- Successfully launch a new product or reposition an existing one

Marketing and advertising directors can't afford to make mistakes. They don't have budgets to waste, and must see great results – now.

I wrote this book for both Presidents and Marketing Directors ... to clarify a path to success for marketing strategies and tactics.

The noise, confusion and overwhelming clutter – ignore them.

The new trend to increase response and achieve greater market response is intelligent, accountable and scientific advertising: multichannel, integrated marketing and advertising.

As a business owner or marketing director, you hear a lot of different advice on how to best market your product or service.

You have learned that social media marketing is a

great route – it's fast, low-cost and relevant.

You might have been told that email marketing is your best option for reaching your ideal audience and getting a high response.

You have also heard about direct mail – an "old school" approach to marketing that gets an excellent response.

Ultimately, you want to implement the best marketing approach – the strategy that will generate a high response at the lowest cost-per-lead and cost-per-sale.

You want to use the approach that will get you the highest profits ... and fastest growth.

For more than 40 years, I've helped businesses achieve rapid growth with marketing and advertising.

I've seen skyrocketing profits.

I've seen ideas and dreams become reality.

I've seen small companies explode into multimillion-dollar companies and large companies grow even bigger.

And, I have learned that the best marketing approach is none of the options listed on the previous page.

It's "all of the above."

This is the very best way to:

- Launch a product or service...
- Grow an existing brand...
- Reposition an existing mature product or service...
- And to dominate your market.

Let me explain:

Your best marketing approach is called "multichannel, integrated marketing."

This approach implements all of the strategies listed above – and more – to significantly boost your response rate … and supercharge your profits.

It's marketing and advertising on steroids. It will revolutionize your marketing results.

Multichannel, integrated marketing is changing the way businesses such as yours reach new prospects … upsell and cross-sell more effectively … get higher response …. and earn massive profits.

Multichannel, integrated marketing:

- Combines marketing across all channels – digital, direct mail, social media and more – to generate new leads, conversions and sales

- Deploys all materials to the same names, boosting response from prospects, leads and current customers

- Drives potential customers back to the same landing page, with the same powerful offer throughout all materials

- Uses advanced data modeling and other high-level targeting strategies to reach your "perfect prospects"

- Gives potential customers the impression and credibility that you have a widespread presence and high budget

And, it's accountable and scientific: You always measure what works and what does not … you know your cost-per-lead and your cost-per-sale.

In the following guide, you'll learn about each aspect of multichannel, integrated marketing … and how you can use this new marketing approach to revolutionize your business.

It's Been Proven: Multichannel, Integrated Marketing Gets the Highest Response

Businesses that use multichannel, integrated marketing report more success and satisfaction with their marketing results than businesses that use a non-integrated, digital-only or single-channel approach.

Though a multichannel, integrated marketing campaign may require more work upfront, it generates more leads and more customers over the long run.

In fact, statistics show that marketers at companies with annual revenues greater than $200 million report that their multichannel, integrated marketing campaigns are three times as effective as other kinds of campaigns.

And I know from many personal experiences, it's the key to success for start-ups or smaller companies.

What makes multichannel, integrated marketing so powerful?

The answer can be found in the graphic on the next page.

As you can see from this wheel of multichannel, integrated marketing, this unique approach uses advanced data modeling and optimized data as the key "starting point" for a marketing campaign.

The ability to specifically target your key target audience with this powerful new data strategy is critical to your success.

It lowers your cost. It enlarges your universe of potential clients or customers. And, it increases your response.

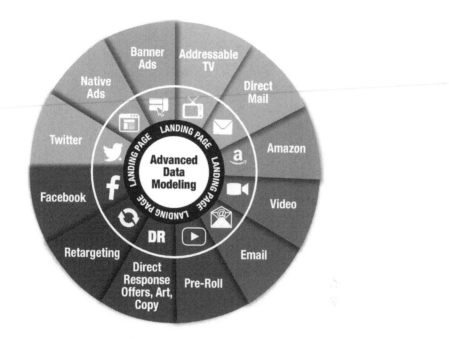

I'll shortly explain why "transactional" data is so powerful in targeting your audience. It's not Google clicks, Facebook likes or other internet data. It's actual buying behavior (see Chapter 2).

This ensures that all marketing materials are targeted at the prospects who are most likely to respond to your offer – and pull out their credit cards to make a purchase.

As you'll see, using this data will transform your marketing and advertising.

It allows you to direct your message across multiple channels so that prospects see your offer many times – and have numerous opportunities to say "yes" to your offer.

These channels may include a combination of any of the following:

A LANDING PAGE

🌐 A powerful, streamlined landing page is the foundation of your campaign. The key is to give your prospects one streamlined call-to-action to respond to your powerful offer.

BANNER ADS

🌐 Banner ads on Google, Yahoo and other platforms are powerful in combination with other media.

DIRECT MAIL

🌐 Direct mail is my #1 "Secret Weapon" for boosting response. Direct mail is essential to most multichannel, integrated campaigns.

AMAZON ADVERTISING

🌐 Amazon marketing is a brand-new strategy that enables you to reach Amazon customers with targeted marketing – even if you don't sell anything on the site.

VIDEO

🌐 Video is a crucial component to your landing page, social media marketing and more.

EMAIL

🌐 Email is used to generate sales and provide response-boosting follow-up to your leads.

PRE-ROLL

🌐 Pre-roll videos are the "commercials before the video" on YouTube and other sites.

FACEBOOK ADVERTISING

🌐 Facebook advertising can be a powerful tool when used correctly ... especially when combined with Facebook Messenger.

TWITTER

🌐 Twitter drives followers back to your landing page with strategically crafted Tweets that sell your product or service.

LINKEDIN

🌐 LinkedIn targets a select audience with your powerful offer through LinkedIn advertising and InMail.

INSTAGRAM

🌐 Instagram is a powerful platform to advertise your offer and increase visibility – and response.

All marketing and advertising materials are "integrated," meaning they work with each other to generate a response by strategically retargeting prospects with the same offer.

Ultimately, every channel receives a higher response than it would by itself.

This phenomenon was discovered and used successfully when Publishers Clearing House began running TV commercials back in the 1980's. They noticed that when they ran these commercials, the response to their direct mail shot up. After all these years, they still do this, because it works.

A typical multichannel, integrated marketing campaign may include the components shown below:

Integrated, multichannel marketing uses multiple components to drive increased response.

Each of these components works together to boost response from prospects, targeting them again and again with your powerful offer and reminding them of the benefits of your product or service.

There are also additional components you might use, such as Amazon ads, a 3-D package, a videolog and more.

A multichannel, integrated campaign might seem complex, but it's actually very simple.

Let me walk you through a typical campaign using these elements, created for an investment newsletter called *Independent Living*.

The writer of *Independent Living* sells a monthly newsletter that helps readers develop wealth-creating investment strategies. By creating multichannel, integrated campaigns to sell his services, I helped this client develop a profit-generating machine that continues to bring in massive revenue year after year, even after we changed the corporate name.

Whether you run a subscription service like *Independent Living* or you sell a one-time product, you can use the same model of multichannel, integrated marketing to boost your profits and response.

Here's a breakdown of the eight core elements we used for *Independent Living*.

1. Data Modeling

Data modeling enlarges your prospect universe for your multichannel, integrated campaign by using advanced transactional data to identify your "perfect prospects." We used this key strategy for *Independent Living* to eliminate wasted dollars on marketing to prospects who won't respond – and massively increase overall response.

2. Landing Page

The landing page is the foundation of the integrated, multichannel marketing campaign. All marketing materials link back to the specially created direct response landing page.

The landing page below, created for *Independent Living*, lists "5 reasons" a prospect would want to invest in a specific opportunity … and then ends with a call-to-action.

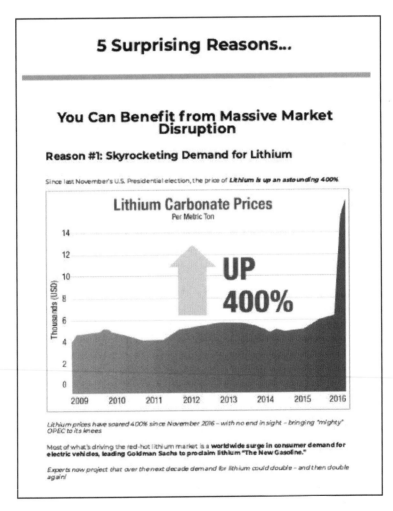

The landing page continued on with four additional reasons, and ended with a call-to-action.

You might notice that this landing page is not like a corporate website; it doesn't have the navigational distractions that could drive prospects away from the page. Instead, it has a single message that brings visitors to a powerful call-to-action at the bottom of the page.

You'll learn more about how to create a powerful landing page in Chapter 24.

3. Direct Mail – Magalog

Direct mail is a key element to an integrated, multichannel marketing campaign. One of the most powerful direct mail pieces you can create to generate response for your campaign is called a "magalog."

A magalog looks like a magazine and feels like a magazine, but it's actually a marketing piece in disguise. For *Independent Living*, I created three direct mail pieces, including this magalog.

A magalog is an ideal strategy for selling a product or service that is a bit more complicated to explain. It can be business to business or consumer. It can drive lead generation or direct sales. It offers the reader valuable, useful information in a magazine-style format that simultaneously persuades them to respond to your offer.

In the magalog shown on the previous page, we used powerful direct response copy to describe a specific investment opportunity – and the amazing benefits of the *Independent Living* newsletter to readers.

This magalog was 20 pages long. I typically create a 16–24 page magalog, which generates a higher response than shorter magalogs. In Chapter 19, you'll discover why longer copy usually leads to more sales, and in Chapter 16, you'll learn more about this revolutionary marketing piece.

4. Direct Mail – Newsalog

Like a magalog, a newsalog is also a marketing piece in disguise. A newsalog looks and feels like a newspaper, but it actually drives prospects to respond to an offer.

For this multichannel, integrated campaign for *Independent Living*, I sent out both a magalog and a newsalog to prospects.

Here's the newsalog I created for the *Independent Living* campaign:

You'll notice that this newsalog has a headline, subheads and articles – just like a real newspaper. The headline reads: "Trump Energy Bombshell," generating curiosity for what's inside.

While newspapers may be going out of business, this "retro-marketing"

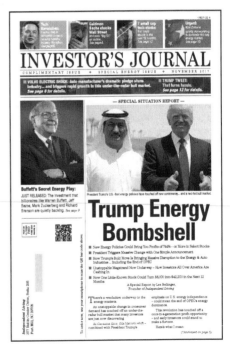

strategy gets amazing response from prospects and customers. In fact, I have seen newsalogs generate a 20-30% boost in response for many of my clients.

You'll learn more about the newsalog in Chapter 17.

5. Email Marketing

For any multichannel, integrated marketing campaign, you can create three different types of integrated, multichannel marketing to maximize response:

1. **Integrated emails** are sent to names who have received the direct mail piece.

2. **Conversion emails** are multiple emails sent to your leads generated from your campaign.

3. **Look-alike prospecting emails** are sent to new leads using a "look-alike" audience based on existing leads.

6. Banner Ads

Banner ads on Google, Yahoo and other platforms are displayed across different websites that prospects may visit. We install a special pixel on the back-end of a landing page to retarget landing page visitors with banner ads.

Independent Living Newsletter

Historic Shift in Consumer Demand Creates Explosive Profit Opportunity

Lithium has been called "The New Gasoline" – and is right now the fastest-growing energy commodity on the planet.

Soaring demand for lithium and the global shift toward electric cars have triggered a historic profit scenario for investors with one little-known "megatrend" stock.

Full Report Here.

Banner ads can be targeted to:

1.Custom audiences

2. Look-alike audiences

3. And as retargeting tools, to leads who have already seen your offer

As you'll discover in Chapter 6, banner ads typically use editorial-style headlines that create curiosity and intrigue in your prospects.

7. Facebook Advertising

Facebook ads run in the newsfeeds of your prospects, shown as ads with a headline, graphic and seven lines of copy.

Like banner ads, Facebook ads can be targeted to custom lists or look-alike audiences ... or be used as retargeting ads.

For *Independent Living*, I created a set of different Facebook ads that advertised their offer and drove prospects to the landing page.

Like all other marketing materials that you create, it is critical that you use direct response copy in your Facebook ads.

Now, you can also display Facebook ads in Facebook Messenger, so that prospects will see your offer displayed in their personal message history. This is a very effective and more direct strategy of reaching prospects, as your ads are not competing with other content for their attention.

I'll cover Facebook advertising in greater detail in Chapter 4.

8. Pre-Roll Ads

Pre-roll ads are short videos that run before longer videos your prospects may watch on YouTube or other video platforms such as Fox News, the Travel Channel or the History Channel. Pre-roll videos get a high response from prospects and leads, especially when they use direct response video technique.

Pre-roll ads can be targeted to custom lists or look-alike audiences ... or be used as retargeting ads.

For the *Independent Living* campaign, we created a special, targeted video to display in pre-roll ads, on the landing page and in other media channels.

Pre-roll videos should not be skipped in your multichannel, integrated marketing campaign. They are an effective tool for increasing your response, and give you a greater degree of credibility. Learn more about pre-roll video in Chapter 11.

What's great is that you can now market with precise accuracy to your client or prospect you're already targeting.

Yes, there are other channels to use for your multichannel, integrated marketing campaign – but as of this writing, they are not as effective. And, there are more to come.

CHAPTER 2

Custom List Targeting Domination

Reaching Your "Perfect Prospects" and Increasing Response and Sales

You might create the perfect multichannel, integrated marketing campaign, with all of the necessary elements, brilliant direct response copy and art and an irresistible offer.

But if it's not targeted to the right prospects, it will fall flat. You won't get a high response, and you'll have thrown away time, money and opportunity.

Targeting is absolutely critical to any marketing campaign.

When I work with a client to create a multichannel, integrated marketing campaign, I ensure that all marketing materials will be directed only at the prospects who are most likely to purchase their product or service.

This could include their own customers and leads in their current database. It could also be focused on prospects who are new to their brand or business.

In either case, I use custom lists for maximum targeting effectiveness – a powerful approach that helps ensure you get the highest possible response to your multichannel, integrated campaign.

Custom Lists: 4 Powerful Segmenting Strategies for Targeting Success

There are four basic types of custom lists that allow you to target specific segments of potential customers, helping to increase overall response and ROI (Return On Investment) across Facebook, Google, YouTube and other digital platforms.

Custom List Strategy #1: Create a List from Your Own Database

First, you can create a powerful custom list simply by segmenting your own database.

For example, you may want to create an ad set for your multichannel, integrated campaign that reaches only your active buyers.

Or, you may want to launch a special campaign to reach former buyers, inviting them to start purchasing your product or service again.

You may want to reach an audience of leads that clicked on an ad for a specific product. You can segment your database to reach this specific audience, with ads to which they are likely to respond.

Here are a few additional examples of audience segments you may want to use to create a custom list:

- ⊕ High-end buyers
- ⊕ High-frequency buyers
- ⊕ Leads from a trade show
- ⊕ Leads from direct mail
- ⊕ People who have visited a specific retail store

As long as you have tagged your contacts and

remained organized in your marketing, you can separate your database in any way you want to create response-boosting custom lists.

Custom List Strategy #2: Target Prospects Not in Your Database to Convert Them to Leads

A second method for using custom lists is to target prospects who are not included in your own database – not leads, current customers or former buyers.

For example, you may want to reach an audience of 100 prospects who are going to a specific trade show or conference. Or, you may want to reach a group of 5,000 people who have been identified as good prospects by an external source. Or, you may use a list of 500,000 or more prospects you have identified.

In any case, this strategy targets prospects outside of your database, expanding your audience and generating new customers.

Custom List Strategy #3: Multichannel Integrated Campaign

You can also create a custom list to strategically market with prospects who have been targeted ... and hitting them with your message in multiple channels.

For example, your custom list can target only those prospects to whom you send emails or direct mail.

These recipients will receive strategic marketing materials from more than one channel.

For example, you could send an email campaign to this list that receives the mailing piece, shown on the next page.

This can work for many specific channels. For example:

- Direct mail
- Email
- Facebook
- Google
- Pre-roll
- Native ads
- Instagram

Each of your targeted prospects will see assets on these channels cross-promoting your products. It seems like you're everywhere your prospect looks.

Custom List Strategy #4: Transactional Data
Custom Lists for Greater "Look-alike" Accuracy

A fourth powerful strategy for creating custom lists is to use advanced transactional data (ATD) to build a new list of your "perfect prospects" and a look-alike audience.

It works like this:

Transactional data is gathered from large database modeling companies, which record thousands of data points of transactional data, such as what a person has purchased over the past six months, year or more; how they make purchases; their income and net worth;

and other information on what they have purchased. Behavioral scientists are then able to "clone" prospects from this information.

Take a look at the following graphic to see what kinds of pieces of transactional data are used by these large companies to identify "the perfect prospect."

For example, the prospect we see below makes $350k a year; spent $150 on a pair of denim jeans in 2017; and donated $750 to animal welfare organizations in 2019.

You'll use this powerful data to reach new prospects, and create "look-alike audiences" to reach more of your "perfect prospects."

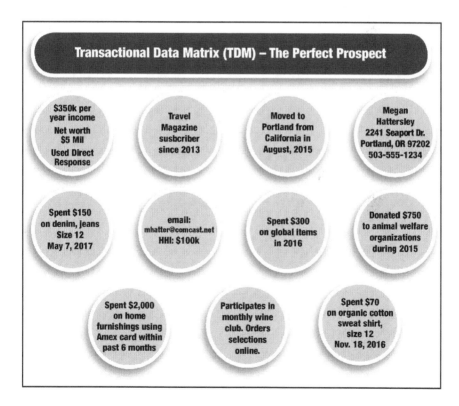

This prospect list then gets:

- Emails
- Direct mail
- Pre-rolls
- Google leads
- Facebook
- Instagram
- And more

This is a far superior strategy to relying on the algorithms of Facebook or other digital platforms, which rely primarily on information such as search history or likes.

Instead, you're reaching prospects who have been reliably proven to have the buying habits that make them ideal customers just for you.

You'll learn more about this strategy in Chapter 3.

Custom lists are critical to your marketing strategy, as they help ensure you are targeting the right prospects with your marketing materials.

They are the backbone of special campaigns that you would want to target on a specific segment of leads or customers.

They are also a powerful method for expanding your prospect universe and generating new leads.

Custom lists should always be part of your multichannel, integrated campaign, as they provide necessary and strategic targeting to maximize your response.

CHAPTER 3

How to Supercharge Your Marketing with Look-alike Audiences

With a perfectly targeted audience, you'll be able to get a high response and generate new leads, customers or clients.

What if I told you that there was a way to reach prospects just like your best customers and leads?

They behave the same, are interested in the same things and share very similar demographics to your most loyal clients.

A look-alike audience, like a custom list, will be one of your most valuable tools in your multichannel, integrated marketing campaign.

If done right, look-alike audiences can dramatically expand your prospects, grow leads and increase the number of your new customers like never before.

There are multiple ways to build a look-alike audience on different platforms.

In this chapter, I'll explain how to create look-alike audiences on the following seven platforms in greater detail:

- Transactional Data
- Facebook
- Google
- AdRoll Prospecting
- Bing
- Pre-Roll
- Amazon

Let's look at how each of these differ ... and how you can supercharge your look-alike quality and response by a little-known strategy I developed for my clients.

#1 Look-alike Audiences Built with Advanced Transactional Data

As you learned about in Chapter 2, you can build look-alike audiences using transactional data, generated from purchases. Using this valuable information, you'll be able to create highly strategic audiences that are virtual clones of your own current customers.

It's so advanced that today I can create a look-alike audience that usually matches 90-95% of the original audience's qualities.

Large database management companies like Oracle store thousands of data tags on prospects. For my clients, I work with behavioral scientists and engineers at their transactional data companies to match them to a precise product or service profile, then create the look-alike audience. It enables us to get a much higher response, doubling it over traditional efforts in some cases.

Using transactional data to build look-alike audiences works especially well if you have a customer list of 5,000 or more names. In this case, the "closing" has been called "miraculous."

#2 Facebook Look-alike Audiences

Another great way to build a look-alike audience is by tapping into Facebook's algorithms. You'll learn more about this in Chapter 4.

Facebook keeps perfecting its ability to duplicate clones of your customers. And while the results aren't as good as transactional data, they come pretty close.

Using these algorithms, I can identify the common qualities of your prospects and find similar audiences on Facebook.

Facebook locates new prospects based on similar profiles and online behavior. What do they click on? What do they like or comment on? Facebook will create a look-alike audience that matches the behavior and the characteristics of the prospects you have identified. This includes analyzing data such as page likes, demographics, interests, website visits and more.

Our very best results occur when I take a model built on transactional data of a customer file and use it as the base audience to create a look-alike audience on Facebook.

You can choose the size of a look-alike audience during the creation process.

A smaller look-alike audience will more closely match your source audience.

Larger audiences increase your potential reach, but reduce the level of similarity between look-alike and source audiences.

However, the larger your customer list or transactional data modeled list the more accurate your look-alike audience will be ... prospects will "look" and behave like your source audience.

And if your source audience is made up of your best customers rather than all of your customers, that could lead to improved results.

#3 Google Similar Audiences

Google uses data collected in the Google Display Network to create a "look-alike" audience. Data includes demographics, searches, video views, website visits, application downloads and more. They use a type of artificial intelligence to analyze trillions of searches and activity across millions of websites to help figure out when people are close to buying.

While a long way from the quality of the transactional data or even Facebook, it's a vital part of any marketing plan.

Again, using advanced transactional data (ATD) and/or your customer files with this approach will dramatically improve results.

#4 AdRoll Prospecting Look-alike Audiences

AdRoll finds audiences using the IntentMap, the largest proprietary data co-op that advertisers can access by contributing their site data.

About 5,000 advertisers of all sizes have opted into IntentMap, pooling more than 1.2 billion digital profiles from across the web and mobile sources.

Such diversity allows AdRoll Prospecting to perform for all verticals and find you prospects.

If you want to make this work even better, use advanced transactional data (ATD) and/or customer data.

#5 Bing Look-alike Audiences

Bing Ads now has a look-alike feature.

Bing's in-market audiences allow marketers to target consumers who appear to be on the verge of making purchases. Grabbing someone's attention when they're ready to purchase is a powerful strategy.

Bing's in-market audiences focus on 14 different targets: four are dedicated to finance, three on travel, two on cars. Others include clothing, hobbies, leisure, toys and games.

And more in-market audience targets are on the way.

#6 Pre-Roll Look-alike Audiences

Having created more than 400 TV commercials and videos, I love integrating video into a campaign. Pre-rolls are a big breakthrough.

You can create a look-alike audience for your pre-roll video on YouTube, using their algorithms. However, you'll get better results with advanced transactional data (ATD) and/or customer lists. This is a powerful strategy to ensure similar audiences see your video ad.

You'll learn more about pre-rolls in Chapter 11.

#7 Amazon Look-alike Audiences

One of the most targeted and effective ways to build a look-alike audience is on Amazon, which I'll cover more in Chapter 9.

Look-alike audiences on Amazon rely on Amazon's own massive transactional data, which creates the most accurate look-alike audience possible.

Look-alike audiences are an extremely effective way to expand reach and target prospects who will respond to your investment opportunity.

Should you use just one platform for look-alike audiences?

No!

I use all seven – and more – and my clients love the results.

For each company and each of the systems, I use slightly different models.

The results of using a look-alike audience include:

- Better Return on Investment (ROI)
- Greater enlargement of the universe

- Higher profits

For these reasons, I use all look-alike audiences. I have one campaign now that's divided 40/20/10 with different look-alike audiences.

One of the keys to success beyond proper testing is knowing how to create the models yourself.

I've learned you should never rely on the modeling company. They are statisticians.

They are not marketers who understand the peculiarities of each target market.

That's why I have trained my staff to modify and adjust each model based on solid direct response psychographic market principles, knowledge and experience.

Building look-alike audiences will significantly elevate your marketing efforts by creating responsive new leads and by powerfully expanding your prospect base.

Part Two

Multichannel, Integrated Opportunities

Multichannel, integrated marketing opens a whole new world of marketing possibilities for your business.

It combines the benefits of every type of marketing – digital marketing, direct mail, TV and more – to supercharge your response.

In Chapters 4–13, you'll discover how to create the online portion of your multichannel, integrated campaign.

You'll discover the secret to effective, strategic Facebook marketing (Chapter 4) ... retargeting your leads with powerful native and banner ads (Chapter 6) ... how to use pre-roll videos to supercharge response (Chapter 11) ... and more.

CHAPTER 4

Facebook Advertising

*Surprising New Integrated Strategies and Tactics on
The World's Most Popular Social Media Platform*

Facebook should be an integral part of a company's integrated, multichannel marketing campaign.

It's profitable by itself.

It's able to lift response to other media.

It's got a variety of strategies and tactics to help you grow.

It's perfect for integrated, multichannel marketing.

Facebook advertising is an effective way to reach the vast majority of U.S. consumers – who, on average, spend 27 minutes a day on this social media platform.

You can precisely target your audience … and it's measurable and accountable.

This gives marketers a great opportunity to reach their most likely buyers with their offer.

Facebook can be extremely effective in increasing your response and boosting your sales.

But it can also fall flat and get you few results … if it's not done right.

Here are two critical keys you must know when using this social media platform:

1. Facebook should not be relied on by itself. It must be used as a part of your multichannel, integrated marketing campaign to maximize return on your investment.

2. In order to get a high response from Facebook ads, you must know important and little-known strategies and tactics.

Let's look at two key strategies:

Lead Generation

Typically, your Facebook ads will drive prospects to your landing page through a "Learn

More" button, such as with the ad shown to the right.

Free Report

Another powerful strategy is to entice prospects to click through by promising them a free report in the body copy of the ad. Here's an example:

I use Facebook advertising for nearly all of my clients and get powerful results from using the following 13 response-boosting strategies...

13 response-boosting strategies to use on Facebook right now

1. Create a custom list.

As I explained in Chapter 2, custom lists are a powerful resource for targeting the right audience – and can be used on Facebook to strategically target and re-target prospects who are likely to purchase from you.

You can upload any custom list – from your existing

database, for example - to Facebook to directly target current customers, inactive customers or new prospects with your offer. For example, you can use a custom list to target leads who have signed up for a newsletter.

You can segment your Facebook custom list any way you want in order to strategically target prospects with specific ads.

Here's a powerful story that demonstrates how effective Facebook custom lists can be in increasing click-through and lead generation.

Volvo's Construction Equipment division (Volvo CE) targeted American and Canadian prospects who were already connected with Volvo competitors.

The company also targeted prospects similar to their current customers, age 23 and older.

The Volvo CE Facebook ad generated 300,000 impressions; 9,485 clicks; and 27 qualified leads.

By using custom lists on this social media platform, Volvo CE was able to bring in $2,000 with every lead … and enjoyed a 30% cost reduction.

2. Create a look-alike audience.

A second key targeting strategy on Facebook advertising is to use your custom lists on Facebook to create "look-alike" audiences, as explained in Chapter 3.

Facebook algorithms are used to review the data and habits of prospects that "look" like your most responsive customers and prospects in terms of their demographics and behavior.

I have developed a strategy to make the look-alike feature of Facebook perform better than the strategies of most digital "experts." It's critical if you don't have a custom/client list. And it helps if you do.

You start with a direct mail transactional model list, create a custom list and then use it to create a Facebook look-alike audience. It's a look-alike audience on steroids.

Here is a Facebook ad I created to target look-alike audiences for a client who was raising capital for his bottled water company.

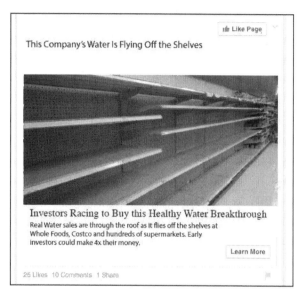

This Company's Water Is Flying Off the Shelves

Investors Racing to Buy this Healthy Water Breakthrough
Real Water sales are through the roof as it flies off the shelves at Whole Foods, Costco and hundreds of supermarkets. Early investors could make 4x their money.

Learn More

26 Likes 10 Comments 1 Share

Look-alike audiences aren't limited to Facebook only – See Chapter 3 for more details.

3. Retarget leads and customers.

Retargeting should not be skipped. Many of your prospects may need multiple touch-points before they will respond to your offer, so it's important to retarget these prospects again with strategic ads.

You'll also want to retarget one-time purchasers or current customers, turning them into loyal, long-term buyers.

Retargeting ads will actually "follow" prospects who have already seen your offer or made a purchase, reappearing in their Facebook news-feeds.

Retargeting ads will not be written like your other advertisements; they should be specifically geared towards prospects who have already seen your offer and may be familiar with your brand or company.

I'll cover retargeting in greater detail in Chapter 7.

4. Facebook "lead ads" allow you to collect contact information.

Facebook "lead ads" are a special type of Facebook ad that allows you to collect the contact information of prospects through a form directly embedded in the ad.

The advantage of Facebook lead ads is that prospects are able to input their information directly on an ad instead of clicking away to a webpage. This is made even easier by the "auto-populate" feature on many browsers.

And, you are more likely to collect the valuable contact information about prospects-turned-leads.

Here is a Facebook lead ad that I created for a client:

When prospects clicked "Sign Up," they would be

taken to the lead form below.

5. Click-to-Call.

Click-to-call ads allow prospects to click a button on your ad that will allow them to immediately call your phone number. Click-to-call ads are ideal for prospects for whom your product or service fills an immediate need (such as a tourism service for people on vacation or food-delivery subscription service for someone who has just moved).

6. Facebook Messenger is a powerful tool.

Facebook messenger allows you to reach prospects directly in their "Messenger" application, which is where they communicate directly with their Facebook friends. Facebook now allows you to run your ads in their Messenger "news-feed," effectively reaching prospects without having to compete with other ads.

You'll discover more about Facebook Messenger in Chapter 5.

7. Follow the rules.

In order to get the most out of your Facebook ads, you must follow certain guidelines, which include:

- **"You-oriented"** copy. Emphasize the reasons why your product or service will change your prospect's life, using words like "you" and "your" frequently in both the body copy and the headline. This is one of the key rules of direct response copy that you will learn about in greater detail in Chapter 19.

Note the copy in this Facebook ad: *Get Your Top Ten Weight Loss Tips*, offering something of immediate value directly to the prospect.

- **Hot words**. You only have limited space in your Facebook ads to create intriguing copy. Use words like "breakthrough," "dramatic," "discover," and "easy" to get your prospects to respond.

In this example, note the power words: "explosive," "historic" and "megatrend."

- **Direct response visuals**. Direct response visuals or graphics are those that get a response. They may not be the most beautiful, but they prompt prospects to respond because they seem "real" or "authentic."

 Powerful video. Video gets a powerful response. When used in a Facebook ad, it can include captions so that prospects can quickly understand your offer and message, even without audio.

By following these time-tested "rules" for all of your Facebook ads, you'll get the most out of your time, effort and money.

8. Create separate ad accounts for different campaign categories.

For example, organize ads for sales of a specific product under its own campaign. The Facebook pixel uses data from previous campaigns to optimize future performance.

To make sure the data gathered from Facebook's pixels best match your offer and creative content, set up ad accounts for your different verticals. Then, organize ads for specific products under their own individual campaign.

When you create separate ad accounts, you can be more strategic in the objective you choose for your ads … and get a much higher response.

9. Write a powerful headline that targets your audience.

70% of your success or failure depends on your headline. Longer headlines get more of a response than shorter headlines.

An effective headline will show the benefits of a product or service. If you have statistics, include them in the headline. Headlines should catch the attention of a reader and pull them into taking action.

Check out the detail-specific headline we created for this investment client (written below the image shown on the right).

10. Create shareable content.

One of the most powerful ways to expand your reach and boost response is to create content that users can share on their own Facebook pages.

Shareable content creates interest and increases curiosity. For example, use a headline that inspires awe in the user. Or, create content that is useful ... for example, "10 Steps to a Healthy Morning Routine."

11. Testing will improve your response rate.

Try testing different headlines, teaser copy and images to improve your results.

On the next page, take a look at the test we ran with different ad copy for a client who sells a weight-loss supplement.

Can you guess which one got the better response?

Ad 1 outperformed Ad 2 by 38%.

Testing is critical to ensure that you get the maximum response on Facebook. You'll learn more about testing in Chapter 28.

Ad 1

Ad 2

12. Use a powerful visual.

If your Facebook ad or post doesn't have a powerful, eye-catching visual, you might quickly lose the attention of your prospect. Use a relevant image that evokes an emotional response.

13. Use a video.

Videos can bring your product or service to life, boosting your response and creating high engagement.

The first few seconds of your video are key. That's your opportunity to capture the attention of your prospective client.

Facebook ads with video allow you to choose a custom "thumbnail image" for the still image that is displayed before the video plays.

Be sure to leverage Facebook's ability to caption videos, too. This will ensure that your videos are more accessible to people who browse with the volume muted. Videos with Facebook subtitles get a 12% higher response. In fact, Facebook's algorithms prefer videos with a subtitle, which will give you a greater reach when you include this feature.

A critical final step: optimize for mobile devices

Just as you must optimize your landing page for viewing on a cell phone, make sure that you optimize all of your Facebook ads for mobile use.

Many of your prospects will be looking at your ads on their cell phones. This means you may have to cut down your copy – and use powerful words and graphics to immediately grab the attention of your prospects as they quickly scroll through their news-feeds.

Take a look at this mobile-optimized Facebook ad I created, on the next page.

You'll learn more about optimizing for mobile phones in Chapter 13.

Facebook advertising will be a critical part of your multichannel, integrated campaign. When used with the key principles and strategies outlined above, it's a powerful way to communicate your offer – and get a profit-boosting response.

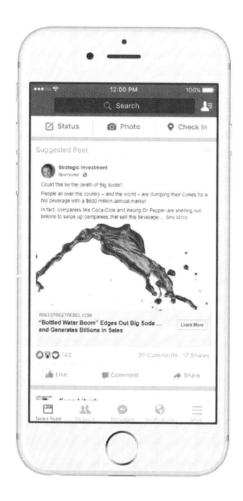

CHAPTER 5

The Facebook Messaging Revolution

In Chapter 4, you learned about cutting-edge, innovative strategies to use on Facebook that will improve response to your multichannel, integrated marketing campaign.

Now, you'll discover one of my favorite tools to use on Facebook right now to reach new prospects and generate leads like never before...

It's so powerful that I have dedicated this entire chapter to it.

It's Facebook Messenger, and it allows you to reach leads and prospects directly with your digital ads ... without competing with the noise and clutter of other ads.

Plus, it helps you build valuable, response-boosting relationships with your prospects and leads.

If you're not completely familiar with Facebook Messenger, it's a stand-alone application that is connected to your Facebook account. Even if prospects don't use Facebook on their phones or other devices, they may use Facebook Messenger. In fact, Facebook Messenger is the #1 app in the iTunes App Store ... while Facebook is #2.

Facebook Messenger may be a critical part of your multichannel, integrated marketing campaign.

The most common way to use Facebook Messenger for marketing your offer is to leverage your existing ads.

When you create an ad, you can "opt in" for additional placement in Messenger.

Here's what an ad in Facebook Messenger looks like:

A second method for reaching prospects and leads directly with Facebook Messenger is to conduct a Facebook Messenger campaign similar to a texting campaign.

Here are six insights and strategies that will help you use this revolutionary new tool to supercharge your marketing now:

#1: Messaging apps get a response that is 10 times higher than response to email or traditional text messaging.

And, users are 53% more likely to buy from you if they can directly message you.

When prospects receive a message on Facebook Messenger, they instantly receive a notification on their cell phone or other device. This increases the likelihood that they'll look at your message – plus, it feels more personal, and increases overall response rate.

#2: Facebook messaging gives users more control.

Users must give businesses permission to communicate with them on Facebook Messenger.

You can only message someone who has "liked" your

page on Facebook, or who has "opted in" through a link on your landing page or email. That means users have more control over who contacts them ... and will be more responsive to your offer.

#3: Use direct response copy.

Facebook Messenger is about creating a two-way conversation. Use direct response copy to address your prospects with "you-oriented" copy and emphasize how your product or service will benefit them.

Your messaging and copy should be personal. Message prospects as if you're speaking to a friend or family member. For example, don't send a free promo code; instead, say, "I saw something you might like..."

#4: "Chatbots" can be used to engage prospects on Facebook Messenger.

Chatbots can actually have conversations with prospects, by answering their specific questions. This makes the whole experience more personal and user-friendly – and it automates the conversation for you.

#5: Ad copy should be short, sweet and direct.

Along with keeping direct response principles in mind, keep your copy brief. Remember, your ads must be optimized for mobile devices ... they occupy a small space, so copy must be short.

Remember, Facebook Messenger is about creating a dialogue. Use direct response copy to address your prospects with "you-oriented" copy and emphasize how your product or service will benefit them.

#6: Run separate ad campaigns for specific promotions or goals.

Try running different campaigns for different goals or objectives. This allows you to gather targeted data about prospects that can be used to further improve future campaigns.

Make sure that all assets in your campaigns are mobile-optimized. That means fewer form fields, shorter copy and streamlined landing pages.

Facebook Messenger offers you a tremendous opportunity to grow new leads and get a higher response to your offer. It overcomes some of the problems associated with email and text-messaging marketing, gives your prospects a personal, user-friendly experience and builds valuable loyalty and trust.

CHAPTER 6

Banner Ads and Native Ads: Your Keys to Effective Lead-Generation or Sales

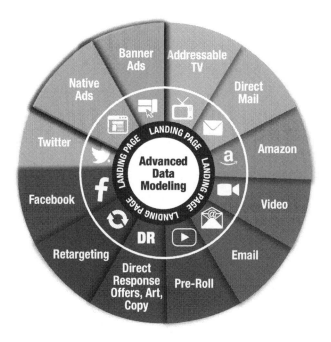

Banner ads and native ads are two types of digital ads that I use for almost every multichannel, integrated marketing campaign.

In this chapter, I'll explain how to create powerful banner ads and native ads. I'll also show you how to strategically target and retarget these ads to prospects and leads, driving traffic back to your landing page and boosting your overall response.

Three Key Marketing Categories for Banner and Native Ads

Banner ads and native ads can be grouped into three major targeting categories for marketing purposes:

1. Custom. Ads targeted to custom audiences will be viewed by a specific custom list that you upload to Google or other advertising platform. You can learn more about custom lists in Chapter 2.

2. Look-alike. Ads targeted to a look-alike audience will reach potential buyers who "look like" your current customers and best prospects. You can learn more about look-alike audiences in Chapter 3.

3. Retargeting. Retargeting ads will be seen by leads who have already visited your website, or started the purchasing process. These ads will lift response significantly by driving leads back to your page to say "yes" to your offer. You'll learn more about retargeting at the end of this chapter.

Banner Ads

Banner ads might appear on various websites that your prospects or leads visit. They include a headline, short body copy, a small image and a call-to-action (CTA) button.

Typically, banner ads have headlines that sound more "editorial." They provoke curiosity by presenting an unusual situation or opportunity.

For example, for a client who writes an investment newsletter, I might create a headline that presents an unusual new investment opportunity:

"The Death of OPEC? Massive Market Disruption Ahead"

Then, I use the brief body copy to explain further… perhaps giving an estimate of how much investors could make on this "newsworthy" opportunity.

To motivate prospects and leads to click on the site, I promise a free special report – a "value-added" piece they can see if they proceed to the landing page.

Native Ads

Native ads are different from banner ads because they look "native" to the surrounding content – that is, prospects may not initially realize they are even advertisements because they blend in with surrounding content.

Like banner ads, they also include a headline, body copy and an image.

Similarly to banner ads, the amount of copy you can create for a native ad is limited. That's why you must use powerful words and create intrigue to compel prospects to click on the ad..

3 Keys to Creating Banner Ads and Native Ads that Get a Response

1. Longer headlines get a higher response than shorter headlines.

The first thing anyone will notice about your banner ad or native ad is the headline. About 70% of the success or failure of your ad relies on the headline.

A weak headline will be ignored and overlooked, while a strong headline can draw in prospects and supercharge your response.

It may seem counterintuitive, but more words and characters often means more click-throughs for your online ads. In fact, headlines between 90 and 99 characters received a click-through rate that was 43% higher than headlines that had fewer than 90 characters.

Take a look at the following test:

Headline #1:

97% of men suffer from some type of prostate problem, but … these amazing nutrients could help you join the 3% who live worry-free!

Headline #2:

Breakthrough Prostate remedy taps decades of scientific research, brings relief in as little as 30 days!

Headline #2 got a 79% higher response.

2. Test, test, test.

Test different headlines, ad placements and graphics to see which variables perform best in your banner ads and native ads.

Testing is the backbone of direct response marketing – testing ensures that the results from your marketing spend are measurable.

Here's an example of a test that measured results from two banner ads, with different headlines and graphics.

(continues on next page)

You'll learn more about testing in Chapter 28.

3. Media strategy.

Banner ads and native ads are only as good as where you place them. You must make sure you are placing them appropriately. Test! Don't rely on Google or a service to do this for you. Evaluate each media placement for its effectiveness.

Retargeting: A Critical Strategy for Increasing Response

Retargeting is absolutely critical to your banner ad and native ad strategies.

Without retargeting your ads, you'll miss out on gaining valuable leads and prospects who may have missed out on your offer the first time around ... but who will respond to the second or third touchpoint.

Retargeting means that your ads "follow" your prospects and leads around the internet: popping up on search engines and different websites.

In order to retarget, you'll need to place "cookies"

on your landing page that tag visitors and direct your ads to follow these visitors.

Here's an example of a "retargeting" banner ad, targeted at a prospect who has visited the landing page, but hasn't responded to the offer.

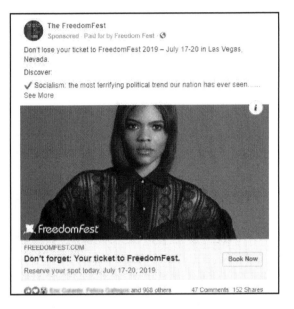

Banner ads and native ads are essential to your multichannel, integrated marketing campaign. They not only expand your prospect base, they are key to your retargeting strategy, which I'll cover more in Chapter 7.

CHAPTER 7

Retargeting to Dramatically Boost Response

A key component of your multichannel, integrated marketing campaign will be to retarget prospects who have already responded to your ads, visited your landing page or purchased your product or service.

In this chapter, I'll dive deeper into the details of retargeting banner, native, Facebook, pre-roll ads and more described in previous chapters.

Why Retarget?

When used by themselves, Facebook ads, banner ads and pre-roll ads can be effective. But when combined with retargeting, they can dramatically increase your number of leads and customers.

In fact, retargeting can result in a 100% increase in click-through for digital ads. Retargeting is the type of banner ad or Facebook campaign that gets the highest response.

Retargeting will also lower your overall marketing cost-per-lead and cost-per-sale.

In some marketing campaigns, 70% or more of landing page visitors will leave without making a purchase.

Even if they start the buying process, nearly the same percentage will abandon your shopping cart before they make a purchase.

Retargeting ads help you get these prospects back to

your landing page or shopping cart and convert them to paying customers.

For prospects who have purchased something from you, retargeting can turn one-time buyers into loyal, long-term customers. You can also use retargeting to turn your one-time buyers into loyal "up-sell" or "cross-sell" clients.

So, how is retargeting done?

Here's how I do it for a multichannel, integrated marketing campaign:

I create specific ads aimed at prospects who have already visited your landing page. The ad is compatible with the direct mail, email or other media message used in the campaign.

When prospects come to your landing page – whether through direct mail, email or other media – I use retargeting codes on the landing page so that your specific retargeting ad will "follow" them around the internet.

For example, they might see a retargeting ad appear on various websites they visit, or in their Facebook news-feed.

This is a powerful way to reinforce your offer and remind prospects of what they showed interest in.

But to make retargeting work at its best, the ad needs to use powerful direct response copy. As explained in Chapter 6 on banner ads, I usually create an editorial looking ad to generate a higher response.

Your offer and/or call-to-action (CTA) are critical to the ad. For example, you may want to show a video and offer a free special report. In any case, you should test to see what kind of offer will work best for you.

Here are some retargeting ads I created that have proven to successfully remarket offers for a conference for libertarians.

A second, critical type of retargeting ad is an ad sent to prospects who started the process of buying your product or service … but abandoned their shopping cart.

These prospects should be re-contacted with a specific kind of retargeting ad, to bring them back to your page to finish the purchase.

You'll discover more about how to decrease shopping cart abandonment with retargeting in Chapter 25.

Here are 12 creative retargeting strategies to use in your ads that will supercharge sales:

#1: Show a picture of the product your prospect searched for to remind them that you have what they need.

You can retarget your prospects with a picture of what they searched for. For example, if your prospect searched for "hearing aids," show a pair of your hearing aids to remind them that they need this product – and yours are readily available to buy.

#2: Remind them to download their "free special report" for value-added incentive.

For many of my clients, I create one or more "special reports" that act as a powerful incentive for prospects to respond as a lead or to buy. If you offer a free special report as a part of your offer, you can retarget leads with a picture of the report – creating curiosity about this free informational piece.

#3: Use a testimonial to prove you're credible and trustworthy.

Show a testimonial of a satisfied customer in your retargeting ad. Testimonials offer powerful proof that your product or service is valuable and can be trusted. Prospects and leads are likely to trust someone else about the quality of your product.

A testimonial can be shown as a video, a special landing page or on your sales page.

#4: Display a video update to create intrigue.

Your landing page should have a video that explains your offer. Create new curiosity and excitement by telling leads that you have a "video update" to take them back to your landing page to watch your video.

#5: Use the word "alert" for response-boosting urgency.

"Alert" creates a sense of urgency, increasing response. "Alert" also suggests you have new, powerful information to share with your leads, helping to funnel them back to your landing page.

#6: Say "thank you" to start a dialogue and create relationship.

Saying "Thank you" creates immediate dialogue with your leads, and reminds them that they have taken action on your landing page. Thank them for their visit, and then remind them about what they forgot to complete (download a free report, buy a product).

#7: Ask a question to bring "shopping cart abandoners" back to your page.

Typically, I don't recommend asking a question in a headline. But when a potential customer has placed something in your shopping cart and then forgotten to buy it, they may just need a reminder: For example, "Did you forget something?"

#8: Tell old customers you miss them to bring them back to your page.

Retarget one-time buyers with ads that say, "We miss you!" This is a powerful way to remind them of your product or service, and create a relationship and trust that can turn them into loyal customers.

#9: "Ready for a refill?" reminds customers to repurchase products they love.

If you sell a product that might be purchased again and again – such as a food or cosmetic product – send a retargeting ad to customers when you think they would have finished the product. For example, if a tube of skin cream lasts a couple of months, send a retargeting ad to a customer towards the end of that cycle that says something like "Ready for more?" or "Ready for a refill?"

#10: "Renew your subscription" turns one-time buyers into continuity buyers.

If you have a subscription service, remind customers to renew their subscriptions with retargeting ads. Or, retarget customers who have canceled their subscriptions.

#11: Ask for a review or testimonial to strengthen your offer.

Retargeting can also be used to get more customer reviews and testimonials, while creating a more powerful relationship with your customers. Soon after a product or service purchase, retarget recent buyers with ads that ask for a review and star rating. For example, "Please, tell us what you think!" with the specific product or service name.

#12: Suggest related products to "upsell."

To upsell your product or service, suggest related items or a larger package to customers, based on their past purchases. Retarget customers with an image of a new, enticing product or service your customer might like.

These are just a few ideas ... but you may come up with additional strategies for your own integrated, multichannel marketing campaign.

Retargeting is a game-changer.

It can dramatically increase your response, help you gain more leads, reinforce your marketing campaign and increase your profits.

It's an essential strategy in your multichannel, integrated marketing campaign.

CHAPTER 8

Email Strategy Now: The Rules of Email are Changing

Email campaigns are an important component of your multichannel, integrated marketing campaign.

However, you must resist the urge to rely on email campaigns alone. Using only email, you will be underperforming – you can do better. But used in conjunction with direct mail and other digital elements, email can help you dramatically lower your cost-per-lead and cost-per-sale.

The rules of email are changing. In the past, it may have been possible to use email alone without having high-level strategy – and still get acceptable results.

But as response and open rates have dropped dramatically over the past 5 to 10 years, you must use email strategically with a different set of rules in order to get a powerful response.

I have sent more than 100 million emails since email became a marketing tool in the late 1990s – and in the process, I have discovered what works, and what doesn't.

For every multichannel, integrated marketing campaign that I create, I design separate email campaigns. These might include two or more of the following:

1. A "prospecting" series. A prospecting series is sent to names on rental email lists who you have no relationship with you and who may have never even heard of you before.

2. A "conversion" series. A conversion series is one of the most powerful ways to turn leads into clients.

With a conversion series, you carry on a conversation – not engage in a sales presentation. Every single email carries on a dialogue. For example, "I forgot to mention. Let me tell you one more thing. It's important for you to note."

It's very personal, one-on-one communication.

It should be used, even if you have a sales team aggressively following up leads.

You may have the very best salesperson trying to call prospects. But the conversion series will get the attention of your prospect, while your salesperson might only get voicemail and avoidance.

If you're giving value to your prospects, they are going to read your emails. They may not be ready for a sale immediately. It may take a week, two weeks, a month, two months, three months or longer – depending on the product or service.

But it's a way to keep in touch with them. A conversion series may include five emails – or it may include up to 18 emails.

Ultimately, a conversion series will maximize your sales results.

3. An "integrated" series. An integrated series is sent to the same names, as a part of the integrated, multichannel campaign. For example, your prospect gets an email, a direct mail package, Facebook ad and pre-roll ad. One tactic is to send an email that gives prospects an idea of what they can expect to receive in their mailboxes, creating curiosity and excitement.

Once recipients actually receive their mailing piece, they receive more "follow-up" emails, with images of the mailing piece about to arrive. Integrated emails reinforce the offer and help persuade direct mail recipients to look carefully at their mailing pieces, with copy like, "Did you see page 2 of your special offer I mailed to your postal box?"

Each of these series might include five to seven emails.

Here is an example of an integrated email that displays a magalog – a direct mail piece that looks like a magazine (see Chapter 16).

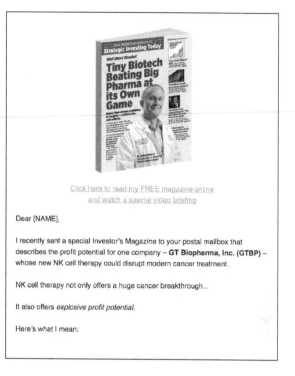

The 3 "R's" of Every Email

Emails flop when they are pure sales-hype. The rules of email have changed. In today's world of spam filters, massive email clutter and little time to read, traditional email sales hype will be deleted. You won't stand a chance.

For every email series that I create (prospecting, conversion or integrated), I follow the "3 R's":

1. Relevant. Every email must be relevant to the needs and the interests of the prospect.

When an email is part of a conversion series, or a retargeting email, the subject line and copy should also allude to something the prospect has already seen.

For example, in an integrated series email sent to a prospect who has received the direct mail piece, I might include "[As seen on pg. 13 of your magalog]" in the subject line.

2. Reputation. Your email series should reinforce your reputation through a proven track record of success. For example, for an investment newsletter writer, I might include details about his track record of anticipating stock market successes in a prospecting or integrated email.

Other reputation-building elements include:

- Written testimonials
- Video testimonials
- Reviews
- Comparison charts
- Star ratings

3. Rewarding. Finally, every email you send must stress the benefits of your offer to the prospect. Your prospects don't want to know about every feature of your product or service; they want to know how it will make them richer, happier, thinner, more successful or younger-looking.

To make an email more rewarding, it should have value. Give valuable information. Teach, instruct or confirm existing beliefs.

Now, let's walk through a breakdown of how

to create a successful email for your multichannel, integrated marketing campaign.

The Subject Line:
The Opener That Can Make All the Difference

Your subject line is absolutely critical to the success of your email. Without an effective subject line, your prospect won't even open your email – and your time, money and effort will be wasted.

In fact, 35% of email recipients have cited the subject line as the most important piece to motivating them to open an email. And, with 269 billion emails sent each day – and your prospect potentially receiving 100+ emails – your email subject line must stand out.

Cute, dull and bland subject lines won't work. Be intriguing, make a promise and create curiosity.

The goal of the subject line is to entice your prospect to read further. Nothing more.

Write 10 to 20 subject lines for each email before choosing two or more to test.

Even the most experienced digital marketer can guess wrong about what's effective. That's why it's absolutely critical that you test two or three subject lines to see which one will work best.

Unlike so-called marketing "experts," the marketplace is never wrong.

In one test, an integrated email campaign went out to all direct mail (in this case, a magalog that looks like a magazine – Chapter 16) recipients, so that they received the email as a "follow-up" reminder of the powerful offer they saw in the mail.

Subject line A: You should have received this magazine by now

Subject line B: This complimentary magazine should be in your mailbox now

Which subject line performed better?

Subject line A got a 42% higher click-thru rate – showing that a small change can make a big difference.

Lastly, use a consistent "from" line, with the same name and email address every time.

Body of the Email:
Counterintuitive Ways to Get a High Response

One of the key principles of direct response marketing is that "pretty" doesn't always get a high response.

It may seem counterintuitive, but plain text emails get 17% more clicks than HTML-designed emails with lots of graphics. They often receive the same open rates, but when a prospect is focused on a single-link text-based email leading to a single call-to-action, he or she is more likely to click through.

Ultimately, the purpose of the email is to drive prospects back to the landing page by enticing recipients with a "value-added" incentive – a bribe to respond.

A value-added piece needs to be something the prospect perceives as valuable and desirable. It could include a set of special reports or other "free gift." You'll learn more about value-added marketing in Chapter 22.

The idea is that you're offering prospects valuable information – not just driving a sale. Copy that is too sales-heavy will depress response.

Finally, avoid hype. Give customers clear, specific information that's easy to understand, and you'll get an above-average response.

Test Different Lists to Identify Who is Most Likely to Respond

There are three types of email lists you can use for email series:

Prospect List

A prospect list is a list that you can rent for a one-time use. If you want to use those specific names again, you'll have to get permission or rent it again.

A prospect list may produce a lot of leads and sales. Or, it may not work. That's why you must test a small portion of the list and see if it works for you.

Integrated List

Your integrated list could include customers, leads or prospects.

These prospects will see your email ... as well as Facebook ads, banner ads, pre-roll ads and other digital ads – all integrated with your marketing message.

Your Own Email List

The last type of email list is your own email list – leads generated by your own database.

For one client, I did a 2-way test with the same email campaign to see which list worked best out of the following:

List "A" = New opens from leads who have previously opened (last 6 months opens)

List "B" = New opens from prospects who have never opened (last 6 months)

The results were as follows:

A...45.33% opens/7.71% click-thru

B...0.97% opens/11.32% click-thru

As you can see, List A received dramatically better results. People who have previously opened your emails

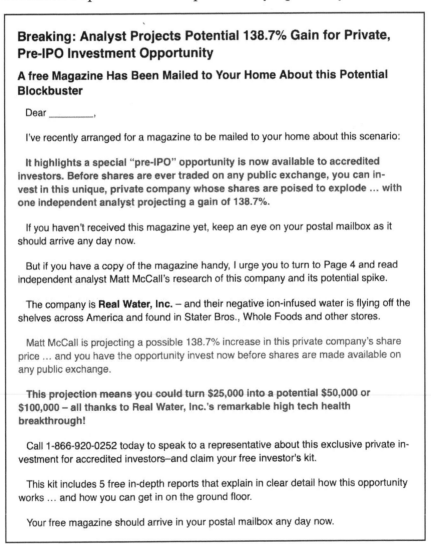

Breaking: Analyst Projects Potential 138.7% Gain for Private, Pre-IPO Investment Opportunity

A free Magazine Has Been Mailed to Your Home About this Potential Blockbuster

Dear _____,

I've recently arranged for a magazine to be mailed to your home about this scenario:

It highlights a special "pre-IPO" opportunity is now available to accredited investors. Before shares are ever traded on any public exchange, you can invest in this unique, private company whose shares are poised to explode ... with one independent analyst projecting a gain of 138.7%.

If you haven't received this magazine yet, keep an eye on your postal mailbox as it should arrive any day now.

But if you have a copy of the magazine handy, I urge you to turn to Page 4 and read independent analyst Matt McCall's research of this company and its potential spike.

The company is **Real Water, Inc.** – and their negative ion-infused water is flying off the shelves across America and found in Stater Bros., Whole Foods and other stores.

Matt McCall is projecting a possible 138.7% increase in this private company's share price ... and you have the opportunity invest now before shares are made available on any public exchange.

This projection means you could turn $25,000 into a potential $50,000 or $100,000 – all thanks to Real Water, Inc.'s remarkable high tech health breakthrough!

Call 1-866-920-0252 today to speak to a representative about this exclusive private investment for accredited investors–and claim your free investor's kit.

This kit includes 5 free in-depth reports that explain in clear detail how this opportunity works ... and how you can get in on the ground floor.

Your free magazine should arrive in your postal mailbox any day now.

are far more likely to open again.

Think twice about deleting inactive names – 24% of your inactive names will open your re-engagement email, and 45% will open emails following.

On the following pages, you'll discover examples of emails I created for multichannel, integrated campaigns for clients.

Real Water

Real Water is a client who was raising investment capital for his alkaline water company.

Note that the email on the previous page is easy to scan and presents the most important information at the top. It also includes a graphic of the direct mail piece that email recipients would have also received in the mail, reinforcing the offer.

The email ultimately asks recipients to respond to the premium or value-added piece, not the offer itself.

Here is another example, from a prospecting series for a weight-loss supplement:

Notice the strong headline, the "you-oriented" copy and the video thumbnail in the

Innovative New Fat Destroyer Makes It Easier for You to Get Rid of Those Stubborn Pounds

Dear Friend,

If you've ever tried to slim down using diet and exercise and haven't gotten the results you want, chances are you're working *way* too hard.

Because recently, I stumbled on a weight loss secret that changes *everything*. In fact, this remarkable discovery can help you lose as much as 24-1/2 pounds of fat in just 90 days!

My name is Jason Berkes — and for more than 25 years I've been uncovering breakthroughs in fitness and nutrition to help you improve your health.

And now, I've prepared a special video that shows you a *much* easier way to get rid of those stubborn pounds...

lose weight and feel great

email.

The email makes the offer clear, and stresses the benefits of this weight loss supplement.

Email series are a powerful way to reinforce your offer and increase response from your prospects.

They are an effective way to increase response and retarget prospects. They also reinforce your mail piece and give prospects another opportunity to respond to your offer.

But they cannot be relied on alone.

Using the keys and principles described in this chapter, you can create effective, persuasive emails that drive prospects to your landing page, ultimately convincing them to click on "Buy Now."

Email is a great marketing tool, but it should never be used by itself. Instead, it should be used to complement other marketing pieces and retarget leads and prospects.

CHAPTER 9

The Amazon Revolution: Nine Powerful Insights and Strategies for This Transformational Marketing Platform

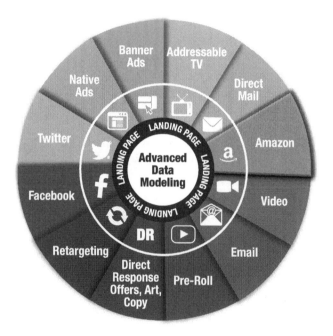

Amazon advertising has become a revolutionary marketing machine.

I'm not talking about selling a product on Amazon. I'm talking about a huge new custom list/look-alike opportunity using Amazon data for an integrated, multichannel campaign.

Harnessing powerful transactional data provided by hundreds of millions of customers, this mega-retailer has dominated the advertising space ... taking from Facebook and Google in the process.

In fact, every time the mega online retailer moves up another percentage point in U.S. retail (worth about $5 trillion), Google and Facebook lose around $50 billion worth of data that they rely on for profits.

Amazon advertising should never be overlooked in your multichannel, integrated marketing campaign.

It will allow you to run highly targeted, effective ads to Amazon's 310 million customer base – even if you don't sell a product on Amazon.

Retargeting: The Foundation of Powerful, Effective Advertising on Amazon

One of the most powerful ways to use Amazon advertising is to retarget your own website visitors with Amazon ads.

The first step is to use a special pixel on your landing page. This pixel allows you to identify prospects who are visiting your landing page and shopping on Amazon ... so that you can see where "audience overlap" occurs on both sites.

When these prospects go to Amazon or anywhere on the web, they'll see your offer advertised, drawing them back to your landing page to respond.

Amazon Look-alike Audiences: A Supercharged Strategy to Expand Your Prospect Universe

Just like Facebook and other social media platforms, you can build a look-alike audience on Amazon using information from the pixel on your site to expand your reach and increase conversion.

Better yet, you can take your custom list to make an Amazon look-alike audience.

Amazon will generate a look-alike audience to generate new leads or customers. They use Amazon's transactional data to reach new prospects or customers that look and behave just like your best customers and prospects.

What makes this better than Google or Facebook and similar platforms is that it doesn't rely on algorithms. It's transactional data, based on real purchases. In other words, it's the most accurate way to generate look-alike audiences that behave – and buy – like your best prospects and customers.

Amazon retargeting and look-alike audiences provide a powerful core foundation for advertising on Amazon. But, there are additional insights you should know to effectively advertise on this powerful site.

Here are nine additional tools to use on the world's most powerful digital retailer – that will help you to grow new leads, expand your customer base and boost profits on Amazon.

#1: Use your own data.

Using your own existing data will not only allow you to create a look-alike audience – it will help you target your current customers and prospects who currently shop on Amazon.

#2: Run targeted ads to your "perfect prospects."

Amazon advertising enables you to create different types of ads for your multichannel, integrated campaign.

Headline search ads

One profitable option for marketers who are selling products on Amazon is headline search ads.

Headline search ads are keyword-targeted cost-per-click search ads that can appear at the top of the first page of search results on Amazon.

Target headline search ads using keywords. Amazon recommends that you use 30 to 40 short, clear keywords.

Display ads

Display ads are targeted, response-boosting ads that can be used to reach customers on or off Amazon. They harness powerful transactional data to target potential leads and customers who are the most likely to respond to your offer. And, they can be used by any business – whether or not you sell a product on Amazon.

Video ads

Video ads on Amazon can be run across the web, displaying your powerful offer in a video. You can run video ads on Amazon regardless of whether or not you sell a product on the site.

You'll discover more about video in Chapter 27.

#3: Access the power of Amazon Prime.

One of the reasons that Amazon advertising is so powerful is that it enables you to reach the vast number of people who are on Amazon Prime, a special paid subscription service that offers free two-day delivery for all subscribers, plus free video streaming services.

Amazon Prime customers are typically frequent shoppers ... and they provide huge amounts of transactional data to Amazon, allowing you to target prospects and customers with even greater effectiveness.

#4: Target prospects and leads based on specific lifestyle demographics.

Amazon will also give you powerful data that allows you to examine the search patterns and browsing habits of specific prospects.

You can identify segments of prospects based on their general lifestyle interests. If you are selling a multivitamin, for example, you'll want to take a look at the buying habits of customers who are interested in health and wellness.

#5: Target customers who have recently searched for a specific product.

You can also use in-market targeting segments to identify and reach customers who have searched for a product in a specific category over the past 30 days. This allows you to target potential customers who are actively searching for products similar to your own.

#6: Lastly, you can target prospects based on general demographics.

Amazon enables you to target audience segments based on general demographics such as gender, age, income and even number of children. This lets you focus solely on your target audience. For example, if you are selling a product for the mature market, you'll want to target consumers ages 55+.

#7: Increase your search ranking by improving relevance.

If you sell a product on Amazon, be strategic about improving your ranking by using keywords. You want your product to show up on page 1, not page 10 ... or 100.

Most products that rank at the top of the page on Amazon are less expensive and higher volume. But even so, you can use specific strategies to improve your ranking.

Like Google, Amazon will not respond to keyword-stuffing or poor word usage.

So, use keywords wisely in your brand name, product-listing title, product description, in the URL, nodes (identified in product category relationships) and product line, which is an additional opportunity to categorize your product.

You can also use keywords in descriptions of color, material, size/dimensions and quantity, as appropriate.

#8: Optimize your product images to maximize response.

Again, if you sell a product on Amazon, you'll want to optimize your product images. Images should be high-resolution, zoomable and shot from a variety of angles. Include product label close-up images; if applicable, photos of the product being used; product shots that show a point of reference, like a hand; and any additional images that might be helpful, like charts or even text.

#9: Run sponsored ads.

Sponsored ads are for those businesses who already

sell a product on Amazon. By pitching your product as a "sponsored product," you can help drive up sales on Amazon.

Sponsored ads are keyword-targeted and are sold on a cost-per-click basis. They can appear on the right side or the bottom of search results on Amazon, or on product detail pages. You can optimize the ad as it runs by viewing clicks or sales. This gives you the ability to maximize the success and performance of your campaign, and decrease the total amount you spend.

Bear in mind, however, that Amazon keeps a percentage of the profits sold by sponsored listings. You should also know that these ads won't link to your landing page for your multichannel, integrated campaign, so they are limited in how you can deliver your powerful marketing message.

By using these powerful strategies and insights, Amazon advertising will become a powerful, response-boosting component to your multichannel, integrated marketing campaign.

CHAPTER 10

Instagram: Your Social Media "Power Tool" for Boosting Response to Your Multichannel, Integrated Marketing Campaign

Instagram is more than just a tool for seeing what your friends are up to or posting beautiful photos.

Think of it as a powerful, far-reaching online catalog that helps you communicate with a wide range of prospects or customers who are likely to respond to your offer.

Not only that, but you can post persuasive video content and even live Instagram "TV" commercials that reinforce your offer.

When used strategically, this social media platform can become an important part of your multichannel, integrated marketing campaign.

There's one very important thing you should know, however. Instagram works best for marketers selling consumer products – especially for those in the health, fitness, beauty, fashion or travel industries.

If that's you, then keep reading to discover seven key insights that you need to know about creating a powerful Instagram campaign to reinforce your offer and boost response.

Key Insight #1: Post frequently.

You must create an Instagram account for your

product. Once you have done so, post frequently to build relationships with your prospects and create interesting and informative content regularly on your account page.

Key Insight #2: Follow direct response principles in your copy and art.

Following direct response principles, your photos and copy should communicate the benefits – not the features – of your product.

You are not limited to using photos alone. You should post graphics and copy as well.

And remember to include a strong call-to-action (CTA) in every post, with a directive to click the "link in bio" to follow through (you cannot include a link in an Instagram post – Instead, links can be included on your account page).

Key Insight #3: Create Instagram stories.

Instagram "stories" are temporary posts that link together into a mini slideshow that your prospects can click on throughout the day.

These are less formal, more casual "live-action" posts that may include video content.

Instagram stories are a powerful way to build an ongoing relationship with your prospects, and increase interest and reach.

Key Insight #4: Interact with your followers.

As you build Instagram followers, interact with them. When they comment on a post, you can reply with a quick "Thank you." This is one of the most powerful aspects of social media – the ability to respond to comments made by others.

Key Insight #5: Instagram TV

Instagram TV (IGTV) allows you to run "commercials" that can be viewed by your prospects.

Your videos can be anywhere from 1 minute to 1 hour long; so if you'd like, you can run a full "infomercial" on this powerful platform. When you upload videos to IGTV, you automatically create a "channel" that can be seen by your followers and a wider audience.

Plus, unlike Instagram stories, IGTV videos remain on your channel – creating a great lineup that your prospects can view again and again.

Once again, this is a powerful strategy for reinforcing your offer and building relationship with your followers.

Key Insight #6: Advertise on Instagram.

Advertising on Instagram is easy when linked to your Facebook account. You're able to quickly and easily sync your Facebook ads to run on Instagram as well, expanding your reach across platforms.

Instagram ads include regular, static photo ads, video ads or carousel ads, which feature multiple, rotating photos.

Instagram advertising is an easy way and effective to reach new prospects, gain interest in your offer and boost response.

Key Insight #7: Instagram "checkout" lets your followers shop directly from the application.

You can include a link to your landing page in your Instagram bio, displayed at the top of your account page.

But now, Instagram followers can also click directly on a post to go straight to checkout and make a quick purchase.

Instagram's in-app checkout feature can significantly increase your overall response rate by making it quick and easy for prospects and customers to say "yes" to your offer.

Instagram could just be the "power tool" that drives up response and profits for your integrated, multichannel marketing campaign. When used strategically to reinforce your offer, it can become a critical key to earning the trust of your prospects.

CHAPTER 11

Pre-Roll Ads: The "Commercial Before the Video"

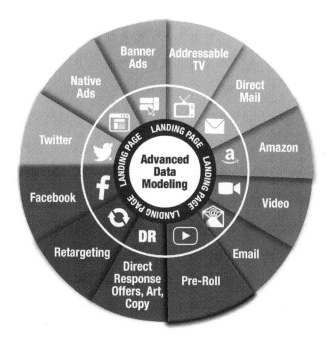

One of the most powerful ways you can use your video is in a pre-roll commercial – it's the "commercial before the video" that you often see on YouTube or another video streaming service.

Pre-rolls are perfect for doing a powerful multichannel, integrated marketing campaign.

They are one of the most effective and rapidly growing techniques being used to target a specific audience, as they get strong response and can significantly grow new leads and prospects.

In fact, they have an average click-through rate of 1.84%. That's higher than any other type of digital ad. And the average online video viewer spends about 16 minutes a month watching video ads.

But here is what is even better:

Pre-roll ads generate leads and sales to grow your business.

And yes, you can also use look-alike audiences with pre-rolls to expand your prospect universe.

4 Strategies Every Marketer Should Use

Here are four strategies to use with pre-roll videos, to boost response rate:

1. Target your best prospects to maximize response.

Pre-roll videos can be targeted to prospects, leads and customers on your custom lists.

Or, you can target them based on specific demographics or lifestyle interests.

Send the pre-roll videos only to those to whom you're sending a direct mail piece, an email, a Google ad or Facebook ad.

It's integrated, multichannel direct marketing at its best.

2. Create pre-roll look-alike audiences to expand your reach.

You can also create look-alike audiences on YouTube to reach new prospects and leads. The best results come from basing the look-alike audience on your custom list of buyers and/or transactional-based direct mail data modeling.

3. Improve SEO with pre-roll videos.

Pre-roll videos give you the added advantage of improved Search Engine Optimization (SEO) on both YouTube and Google, increasing your search ranking and overall visibility.

4. Optimize your pre-roll videos with buttons.

YouTube provides special buttons for pre-roll videos that say, "Shop Now", which can easily be converted to "Subscribe Now", "Donate Now", "Attend This Event", etc. These buttons can help increase your response rate by driving prospects to your landing page with a powerful call-to-action.

Here's a powerful example that shows what kind of response pre-roll videos can achieve:

The Nassau Paradise Island Tourist Board spent more than $1 million on Google TrueView, the platform that enables marketers to run ads on YouTube.

YouTube lets viewers skip ads after five seconds. But, advertisers are only charged if the entire 30 seconds are viewed.

The average completion rate of the Tourist Board's 30-second pre-video commercial rose up to 20%. By the end of the campaign, their price per completed view was only 8 cents – a powerful ROI.

Using these four strategies, you'll be well on your way to creating a powerful pre-roll video that generates new leads and gets a high response to your multichannel, integrated marketing campaign.

CHAPTER 12

Infomercials: Overlooked, But Still Powerful Strategy

I love direct response TV, better known as infomercials. When done well, they can become a powerful part of your multichannel, integrated marketing campaign.

In the early days of television, infomercials exploded in popularity. In fact, many TV shows actually sold sponsored products at the end of the program. When the government cracked down with rules and regulations like the "Fairness Doctrine," however, infomercials were crippled. Many marketers were forced to simply use 30 to 60 second commercial slots.

In 1987, President Ronald Reagan deregulated the airwaves. Once again, marketers were free to advertise with direct response TV. Infomercials exploded in popularity, generating millions of dollars in sales.

I helped my clients take advantage of this massive opportunity, and created powerful infomercials that generated new leads and sales.

We soon learned that infomercials also helped lift response to:

- Direct mail
- Print ads
- Direct sales

And a major benefit: Retailers who routinely said, "NO!" to products completely changed their attitude when infomercials aired. They begged for the product to be sold in their stores, displaying "As Seen on TV" signs throughout their facilities.

Why?

Because the multichannel marketing increased sales and profits, and made products sold on TV credible and desirable.

Today, direct response television in the form of infomercials and commercials is still one of the most effective, cost-efficient ways to reach a large number of prospects, convince them of the value and benefits of your product or service, and convert them into buyers.

You may be thinking, television has changed.

And you're right.

People are watching more TV than ever – but most of it is on streaming television services. Although this presents a new challenge to advertisers, it also creates a great opportunity for direct response marketers.

Because the cost of advertising on cable television continues to go down, direct response marketers now have more opportunities to advertise on traditional television at a lower cost.

Ultimately, direct response television in the form of infomercials will help:

- **Increase sales.** Infomercials sell products directly to consumers and sometimes business to business.

- **Generate leads.** Infomercials can be used to generate prospects. Send these prospects brochures, videos or product samples etc. that will generate direct sales or bring the prospect into their nearest retailer.

- **Gain retail distribution.** Products that might never see retail distribution are fast-tracked to the largest retailers once the infomercial hits.

- **Relationship marketing.** Once you have generated

your leads and built a database, begin developing relationships with your prospects. For instance, send your prospects an unsolicited sample of your product to encourage a purchase.

- **Continuity program.** Once a consumer's business is captured with an initial sale, subscription or club membership, keep your customers buying every month or quarter through installments in a series of catalog or box/subscription sales.

- **Brand awareness.** Infomercials can function in the same way traditional advertisements do, by helping to create and strengthen brand identity.

If you decide that infomercials are right for your multichannel, integrated campaign, you'll want to use specific strategies and tactics to ensure the success of your commercials.

Here are 11 strategies to use now to maximize response to your infomercials:

Strategy #1: Consider your product.

The products that work best in infomercials are those that are easily demonstrated. For example, cosmetics sell well through infomercials because the viewer can see them being applied and how attractive they make the wearer.

Strategy #2: Educate your prospects.

Research shows that the primary reason many prospects do not buy is that they do not have enough information to make an "educated" purchasing decision.

Give your prospects enough information to educate them about products and services. Tests have proven that when there is a substantial amount of information to be communicated about a product or service, 30-minute infomercials work best.

Strategy #3: Motivate the viewer to buy immediately.

Emphasize urgency in your offer by giving prospects a bonus or discount if they buy within a certain time period.

Strategy #4: Present information in an engaging, easy-to-grasp way.

Use a mix of hard facts, expert advice, verification, personal appeal and the testimonials of satisfied customers. These elements should be combined with the visual impact of television to make your product or service irresistible.

Strategy #5: Position yourself without being overtly commercial.

You can use a professional "spokesperson" or celebrity host to guide viewers through your program, interview independent experts and company executives, interact with satisfied customers and provide transitions in between scenes.

Strategy #6: Repeat important claims about your product or service.

Appropriate visual reinforcement should include the use of eye-catching graphics, video effects, stock documentary footage, charts and graphics, star ratings, still photos and dramatic re-creations.

Strategy #7: Use the right music and sound effects.

Music and sound are critical to powerfully enhance key moments in the program and increase product value.

Strategy #8: Design the entire infomercial to "sell" your product or service.

Remember, your commercial is not entertainment; it's an opportunity to drive up sales and make a profit. Use the principles of direct response marketing throughout your entire commercial.

Strategy #9: Emphasize important ordering information.

Make it easy and clear for prospects to order by showing your URL, your Toll-Free number, your text information and other important ordering information on-screen throughout the commercial segments and at other appropriate times throughout the program.

Strategy #10: Be strategic with pricing.

The price of products sold on infomercials is as varied as the products themselves, from $39.00 to over $100,000. However, most are in the $19.95 to $295 range. Many marketers have found their best results come when offering installments, such as four monthly installments of $39 each.

Strategy #11: Make a powerful close.

Last but not least, include a warm summary and a strong call-to-action at the end of the infomercial. Remember, the point is for viewers to immediately respond to your offer when the commercial ends.

Infomercials should become a powerful component of your multichannel, integrated marketing campaign.

They can position your product or service strategically in the marketplace, drive traffic back to your landing page, and most importantly, significantly drive up sales.

CHAPTER 13

Mobile Marketing Breakthrough

Let's face it: Smartphones have taken over the marketing and consumer space. There are more than 2.5 billion smartphone users worldwide, with nearly 247.5 million of those users in the United States alone.

And, in the past six months, 62% of smartphone users have made a purchase online using their phone.

Smartphones are quick, easy and convenient ... and they can be used as powerful marketing tools, especially when used for texting.

However, if your landing page, emails, ads and pre-roll videos aren't optimized for smartphones, you can be sure that your prospects will click away from your marketing immediately ... and you'll lose a lead, a potential customer and sales.

In this chapter, you'll discover how to take advantage of the "smartphone revolution" to succeed in your multichannel, integrated marketing campaign.

Texting for Lead Generation and Data Collection

Texting has revolutionized the marketing space. It allows rapid, direct communication like no other marketing medium ... and can powerfully increase response to your multichannel, integrated marketing campaign.

Here are three ways to use texting to supercharge your multichannel, integrated marketing campaign:

1. Follow up with a text message.

A text message campaign can be a powerful way to follow up with leads who have visited your landing page, or clicked on your ads and provided their phone numbers.

Give prospects another chance to respond to your offer on their smartphones, and see a massive increase in response ... and profits.

2. Send special offers, codes and updates.

Text campaigns are especially effective when they include something of immediate value to your prospect – such as a discount code, coupon or relevant update.

3. Collect valuable data.

Asking your audience to text in order to respond to an offer is also a good way to collect phone numbers from prospects.

Here's a story of how one of my clients used texting for truly phenomenal data collection:

A Christian musician held a concert with thousands of people in the audience. I told him to hold up his cell phone during his performance and ask everyone in the audience to get their phone out as well. Then, we displayed a number to text on the main screen. He asked them to text the number and offered everybody a free download. Thousands of concert-goers took out their cellphones, immediately responded and texted the phone number, providing their email addresses and home addresses as well.

Now, the musician had a new database, and was able to market new albums and releases to them in the future.

Texting campaigns might become a critical strategy for your multichannel, integrated marketing campaign by retargeting prospects, reinforcing your offer and significantly boosting response.

5 Rules for Mobile-Optimizing Your Landing Page

Every digital asset of your multichannel, integrated marketing campaign must be optimized for smartphones.

Here are five rules to follow to ensure that your marketing assets are "mobile-friendly":

1. Write a powerful, benefits-oriented headline.

Mobile users will be viewing your landing page on a small screen that shows less text. So, be sure your landing page includes powerful text upfront. An intriguing, captivating headline will help make sure your prospects continue scrolling through your landing page.

2. Write a list of your key benefits.

Presenting your offer as a "list" is a powerful way to streamline your copy and keep prospects intrigued and interested. Ultimately, this list drives them to your call-to-action to purchase your product or service.

For example, for an alternative health product that utilizes Manuka honey as the core ingredient, you might use the landing page headline "5 Surprising Reasons Manuka Honey Can Transform Your Health." When prospects scroll down, they see five different sections of copy that persuade prospects about the benefits of your offer.

3. Streamline your landing page.

Your landing page must be designed for mobile use. It should be single-column and free of navigational distractions. Your call-to-action (CTA) must be clear, with a one- or two-step process for your shopping cart (for more information on your shopping cart, go to Chapter 25).

4. Cut down your copy.

On a digital ad, your copy may have to be shorter to display correctly.

5. Test, test, test.

Always test. Test your landing pages on different web browsers, as well as a smartphone, laptop and desktop to ensure that they appear correctly, and are clickable.

By following these five rules, you'll optimize your multichannel, integrated campaign for mobile phones – and prevent losing many of your customers … and sales.

Now, I'd like to tell you a story about how mobile marketing can create a phenomenal marketing breakthrough.

Campaign Breakthrough: How Nike Used Mobile Marketing During the Super Bowl to Boost Sales

When done right, mobile marketing can create phenomenal, buzzworthy breakthroughs that can rapidly boost sales.

During the 2018 Super Bowl, Nike outfitted half-time performer Justin Timberlake with a pair of limited edition Air Jordans while he sang and danced in an elaborate performance.

Only minutes after the show, the high-end Nike sneakers – selling for $200 a pair – completely sold out. How did Nike do it?

They followed this six-step plan to maximize their

marketing opportunities on the smartphone, create immediate engagement and achieve a massive spike in sales:

1. Use a high-profile "spokesperson."

By outfitting one of the music industry's biggest stars in a pair of their sneakers, Nike created instant credibility and hype around the Air Jordan III "JTH."

2. Follow the principle of AIDA (Attention, Interest, Desire, Action).

Nike's promotion showcased the marketing principle of AIDA (see Chapter 19 for more details on AIDA) to instantly convert prospects into leads and leads into customers.

First, the flashy white sneakers worn by Timberlake caught the attention of viewers.

Second, the fact that Timberlake was wearing Air Jordans created interest.

Viewers who have a special interest in sneakers and who use Nike's SNKRS app – Nike's ideal audience – would have noticed the new sneaker, which hadn't been released yet on the market. They might have already read about the design of the shoe, which was posted a couple days prior to halftime and cross-linked on the SNKRS app.

Third, as leads were shown strategic shots of the shoes again and again, their desire to buy the shoe was peaked.

Fourth, leads became customers when Nike sent strategic push notifications to their phones marketing the shoe ... and they quickly took action to make a purchase.

3. Use social media strategically.

Pre-show, Timberlake posted a photo of himself wearing the limited edition Jordans on Instagram, in a shot meant to highlight the new shoe. Followers of Timberlake on social media would have immediately seen the photo, helping to create buzz and curiosity.

4. Focus on a targeted audience.

Right after Timberlake's performance, Nike sent a push notification to users of the SNKRS app. The notification – which popped up on the phones of tens of thousands of ideal prospects across the country – sent users to a special landing page to purchase the shoe.

5. Create higher response with a "limited edition" / limited number offer.

Nike created exclusivity – and generated much higher response – by marketing the shoe as limited edition. The shoe sold out in a number of minutes.

Air Jordan III's now sell online for well over their original selling point ... some for as much as $1,000 a pair.

6. Retain leads and increase follow-through with an easy check-out process.

Users who visited Nike's special landing page were led through an easy purchase process: credit card, shipping and shoe size information was pre-populated, so all it took users was a couple clicks to make a purchase.

By facilitating this purchase process, Nike avoided the common problem of shopping cart abandonment.

Prospects were taken to an easy landing page, where they could click on "buy now" to immediately make a purchase.

These six strategies produced a massive marketing success for Nike.

And though not every brand might have the leverage to use high profile stars like Justin Timberlake during an event like the Super Bowl, the steps Nike took can be followed for different kinds of events.

For example, you might leverage the influence of a speaker or musician at a local event to help you sell a product.

By executing the principles and strategies outlined in this chapter, you can use the smartphone and other devices to your advantage – producing surprising results for your multichannel, integrated marketing campaign.

Little-Known Secrets To Using Direct Mail For Multichannel, Integrated Marketing

In Part Three, you'll discover one of the most underrated – and most powerful– types of marketing: direct mail.

Direct mail gets a phenomenal response.

And while your upfront cost may be higher, your ROI will be worth it.

In Chapters 14–18, you'll learn specific strategies, formats and tried-and-true techniques for creating a direct mail campaign that complements your digital campaign…for skyrocketing response – and profits.

CHAPTER 14

Direct Mail Resurgence: Your "Secret Weapon" for Getting an Exceptionally High Profit-Boosting Response

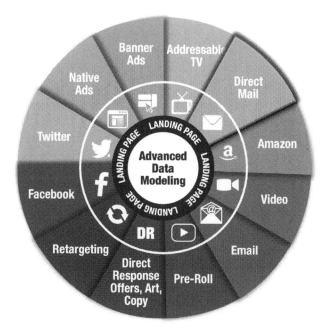

Your landing page, banner ads, Facebook ads, Amazon ads and email are all valuable media for targeting your audience.

However, your #1 media for reaching prospects with your offer is direct mail.

Yes, it may sound "old school"... but direct mail

remains extremely effective in generating high-quality leads that will convert your prospects into loyal customers.

No other component of marketing can target your "perfect prospects" quite as well and specifically as direct mail.

This marketing medium may require a larger investment upfront ... but in the end, you'll get a lower cost-per-lead and cost-per-sale because of the significantly higher response rate.

In this chapter, you'll discover why direct mail is so powerful ... and how this marketing medium can be targeted to generate responsive leads for your multichannel, integrated marketing campaign.

The Power of Direct Mail in an Online World

Direct mail gets an amazing response ... if done right. Why?

- It's ideal for a multichannel, integrated marketing campaign. Direct mail can be integrated with your digital assets for powerful results.

- It's highly targeted. Direct mail can strategically target your prospects, leads, former customers, current customers and prospects. For prospects, a relatively new tactic that works well is using advanced modeling based on transactional data ... The targeting includes mailing only to those who are direct mail responsive and never mailing to those who are not.

- It's powerful and compelling. A direct mail piece makes a high impact. Direct mail pieces usually contain longer copy and more information than other marketing materials, effectively and powerfully persuading prospects to respond to your offer.

◉ It builds trust and a relationship. Direct mail pieces convey a personal touch and special value that help foster a relationship with the prospect.

Direct mail is very effective ... but it should be integrated with other elements in your campaign to maximize response.

Using Direct Mail in Your Multichannel, Integrated Marketing Campaign

Direct mail integration with digital elements in your multichannel campaign will dramatically increase conversion and the return on your investment (ROI).

Here's how I integrate non-digital marketing material with digital elements:

1. Data. First, I use advanced data modeling to identify the names of direct mail recipients who will be most likely to respond to a specific offer. Using the transactional data matrix (TDM), I'm able to target prospects based on their actual purchasing history. Then, I target these same prospects on the internet, with digital marketing assets such as email, Facebook ads and other types of communications.

2. Drive direct mail recipients back to the landing page. Prospects who click on digital marketing materials like ads and emails will be directed back to a single, streamlined landing page, where they will see the same offer they saw in their direct mail piece. The direct mail piece will also include the URL of your landing page, so they can visit it directly after receiving their mail.

3. A single, powerful offer is reinforced on both pieces. Direct mail and digital marketing assets all include the same messaging, working together to reinforce each other. For example, Facebook ads, banner ads and native ads that target direct mail recipients remind them of what they've already seen in the mail – "Did you see this on page 7 of your free magazine?"

Again, prospects are driven back to the landing page, where they are more likely to respond to the offer.

4. Follow up the direct mail piece with an integrated email series. Direct mail recipients not only see digital ads reminding them of the offer; they also receive an integrated email series that reinforces the direct mail piece.

Prospects receive at least one email before they get their mailing piece, with an image of what they can expect to find in their mailbox and copy to create intrigue.

Then, they receive several follow-up emails after they receive their direct mail piece containing subject lines like "Did you see page 12 of your free magazine?"

5. Use direct mail retargeting. One of the great new revolutions in direct mail and online marketing is called direct mail retargeting (DMRT).

DMRT allows you to identify the physical mailing addresses of your landing page visitors, which allows you to send them a direct mail piece … within 24 hours.

DMRT is a game-changer. It allows you to immediately retarget hot prospects with your offer, and communicate with them in a powerful direct mail piece.

The Lost Art of Great Return on Investment (ROI)

In direct mail, oftentimes an envelope mailing with a long letter will often produce better results than an envelope mailing with a short letter.

Likewise, a 20-page magalog or newsalog often gets a better response than a 16-page envelope mailing piece. The cost and the length of the piece may be higher ... but ultimately, your ROI will also be higher.

Having good ROI results from executing a multichannel, integrated campaign that will get you the results you're looking for – a high response with both a low cost-per-lead and cost-per-sale.

And with scientific and measurable direct mail, you're always able to determine the ROI.

You might also benefit by investing money upfront in direct mail programs.

In fact, for every $167 spent on direct mail, marketers sell $2,095 in goods.

Here's an interesting test that demonstrates why a larger investment upfront may produce superior results:

Harry and Joe both published a travel newsletter for budget-minded travelers. They both decided to use a 50,000-piece direct mail campaign to attract new subscribers.

Harry decided he would execute his direct mail campaign on a postcard. After printing and postage, Harry paid $0.47 per postcard and he received 200 leads for a 0.4% response rate.

Joe decided to take a different approach in his direct mail campaign. He created a direct mail campaign using a traditional direct mail envelope package. He generated 950 leads for a response rate of 1.9%, but each of his pieces cost him 11 cents more, at $0.58 a piece.

Who made the smarter investment?

The postcard mailing was in fact cheaper, but when the figures were in, it cost $117.50 per lead. Although the envelope mailing was more expensive upfront, the cost per lead was $30.53. In the end, the postcard mailing was much, much more expensive if you factor in the response rate.

This test demonstrates why it's very important to test your mailing piece not simply for results or cost, but for its ROI.

For example, a #10 envelope is the least expensive envelope you can use … but it doesn't always get the best results.

In the past, I used 9x12 envelopes for clients that have worked very well. Unfortunately, the post office now adds a postal penalty for this size envelope.

A 6x9 envelope with a four-color, powerful sales message will often get a great response – and a great ROI.

Direct Response vs. All Other Approaches

General ad agencies often produce "image-based" direct mail. It looks pretty. But it doesn't produce a response.

The only approach you should use in your direct mail sales piece is direct response – not a mailing based on image alone.

Direct response marketing relies on powerful, benefit-oriented copy that speaks directly to the reader.

You could lose 5-10 pounds in as little as one week.

You'll regain energy and confidence like you've never had before.

You won't want to miss this opportunity to reap soaring profits.

Direct response copy relies on a set of proven rules that generate content that gets a response.

Beautiful graphics and cute copy might look great on your direct mail piece ... but they won't get people to pull out their credit cards.

Your copy and graphics must adhere to direct response rules – or your direct mail piece will fall flat and you'll waste your time and money.

I'll explain this scientific, proven approach to copy more in Chapter 19.

CHAPTER 15

Traditional Envelope Direct Mail – Little-Known Strategy for Skyrocketing Profits

In the previous chapter, you learned about the exceptional power of direct mail to generate leads and boost response.

In this chapter, you'll discover how to create high-impact, powerful direct mail pieces.

You will also learn about the different direct mail formats you can use to communicate your powerful offer.

6 Critical Keys to Direct Mail Success

I've overseen the creation and mailing of more than 1 billion direct mail pieces that have helped our clients dramatically expand their customer base and boost their revenue, sometimes growing from small companies into multimillion-dollar businesses.

After four decades and testing more than 10,000 variables, I've identified and developed six critical keys to success using direct mail:

#1: Targeted Mailing Lists

The best mailing list targets only the most likely prospects with the best postal mailing list filters. It's a major reason direct mail can be so much more effective than online marketing. This means using advanced transactional data modeling for targeting the right prospects. If you need help with this, I recommend you contact InfoMat at (310) 212-5944 for guidance.

#2: Proven Direct Response Copy

The right direct response copy is the most important and overlooked difference between success and failure. Use only direct response copy in your direct mail campaigns and see a massive response (see Chapter 19).

#3: A Compelling Offer

A compelling, benefit-driven offer is a key to success. Your offer must entice the prospect to respond by telling them how your product or service will improve his or her life (see Chapter 21).

#4: An Effective Landing Page

Your direct mail package drives your prospects to your landing page. If your landing page doesn't follow the principles outlined in Chapter 24, you're not going to get the great response you're looking for.

#5: Aggressive Follow-up

Follow-up with leads ensures smart conversion. This step is essential, no matter how good your business opportunity is. Follow-up includes retargeting ads and creating an integrated email series.

#6: Analyze Your Results

Analyzing your results helps you to improve your campaign and continually produce better results.

You need to always know your "cost-per-lead" and "cost-per-sale." This is scientific advertising. Done right, direct mail will generate a lower cost per lead and lower cost per sale than any other medium.

These six critical keys provide a good foundation for a successful direct mail piece.

Let's take a closer look at the first two keys of direct

mail success: laser-sharp targeting with postal lists and dynamic direct mail formats.

Precise Targeting for a Supercharged Response

One of the reasons direct mail is so effective is because of its unmatched ability to target precisely. Other kinds of media lack this precision.

Advanced data modeling and postal lists target your "perfect prospects" – those contacts who are most likely to respond to your offer.

Postal Lists

Depending on your product or service, postal lists can be used to target people in a certain demographic, or who have exhibited certain buying behaviors before.

When I choose postal lists for clients, I always look at R.F.M.:

Recency. The more recent the names, the better the response.

Frequency. The more they respond to different direct mail offers, the better the name.

Monetary. The more they have paid, the better the prospect's response will be.

These are predictors of how well a campaign will work.

With every campaign using direct mail, I analyze which lists are producing the most response to each type of offer and promotion. This critical database of response helps us to avoid wasting resources and ensures that we use the very best lists.

Data Modeling

Data modeling can be used to generate names of the "perfect prospects" who will respond to your offer. These names are generated by assessing massive amounts of transactional data that's collected by database modeling companies (for more on data modeling, go to Chapter 2).

Modeled data will generate a much higher response than non-modeled data.

Take a look at the graphic below to see the difference.

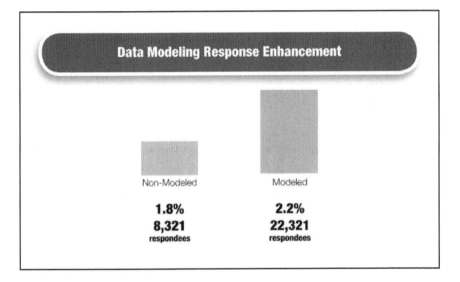

Data Modeling Response Enhancement

Non-Modeled
1.8%
8,321
respondees

Modeled
2.2%
22,321
respondees

Here are examples of list segments where you can select more targeted data for a direct mail campaign:

- Male or female
- Living in a home or an apartment
- Geographic area — region, state or local ZIP codes
- Income levels or net-worth levels
- Direct mail responsive

- Like sports, gardening, travel, music and other interest variables

- R.F.M. (Recency, Frequency, Monetary)

When selected carefully, these test segments help you to identify your most responsive leads.

Using these targeting techniques, you can reap the rewards of this marketing medium's exceptional targeting ability.

But in order to maximize the impact of direct mail in your multichannel, integrated marketing campaign, you must choose a strategic direct mail format that best fits the needs of your prospects.

Strategy: Choosing the Best Direct Mail Formats for Your Campaign

A variety of direct mail formats can be used for a successful direct mail program.

Here's an overview of the types of formats that will help you to create a high-impact direct mail campaign that delivers a powerful response:

- **Traditional direct mail package.** This is a mailing package with a letter, lift note and response device inside an envelope.

- **Magalog.** A magalog looks and feels like a magazine, but it's actually a direct response sales piece, designed to generate interest and response in your product or service.

- **Newsalog.** Like magalogs, this is a powerful direct mail format that can help dramatically raise response. It looks like a newspaper. It feels like a newspaper. But it's really an advertisement for your product or service.

- **Bookalog.** A bookalog is a book that acts as an informational and advertorial piece to the investor.
- **Three-dimensional (3-D) package.** If you're doing a highly select campaign to a small audience of fewer than 10,000, I often recommend doing a three-dimensional piece.
- **Videolog.** This is high-tech direct mail at its best for an audience of fewer than 15,000 people.

Let's take a closer look at these six key formats for direct mail...

Traditional Direct Mail Package

A traditional direct mail package is a powerful way to generate leads and sales.

Traditional direct mail, if done right, can generate high-quality leads for your offer. I recommend direct mail if your product or service is clear and easy to understand.

If your offer is more complicated, I suggest using the magalog, bookalog or a three-dimensional piece described on the following pages.

The traditional direct mail package usually consists of these components:

Envelope

You might be inclined to ignore the envelope, but this is one of the most crucial pieces of your direct mail package. Why? A powerful envelope has one purpose: to get the prospect to open it.

If the envelope doesn't immediately catch the attention of the recipient, it won't be opened and your direct mail package will be wasted on a potential customer.

A powerful envelope can be handwritten or personally typed, with high-quality personalization. I use a special machine that will "handwrite" using a pen – a method called "real pen."

With "real pen," a computer engraves writing on your envelope, but it looks like a person did it.

Teaser Copy

Copy on the envelope – called teaser copy – will usually produce better response than a blank envelope.

And – though it might seem counterintuitive – copy on the back of the envelope can increase response by as much as 15%.

I always test to see what type of envelope will perform best in any specific marketplace.

Take a look at the following examples of envelopes I've used in different integrated, multichannel marketing campaigns.

The first example shown below is an envelope I produced for a company that marketed an investment opportunity in rare gold coins.

On the next example, notice that the name and address appear to be handwritten. This is an example of an envelope with computer-generated "handwriting." This can be an extremely effective method of getting your envelope opened.

Notice the "handwritten" request below the name and address on the example above. This detail can make the difference between a direct mail package that is responded to and a package that is completely ignored.

Here's an envelope I created for the Pacific Justice Institute, a legal advocacy non-profit:

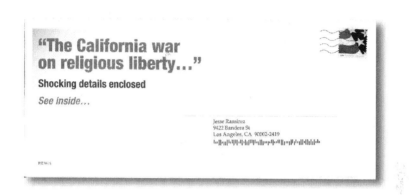

Here is an envelope with teaser copy that immediately defines the unique selling proposition (USP) of the offer: "The banker's secret to potentially making...7%-10% yearly returns...paid to you monthly."

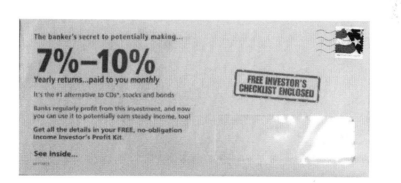

Finally, here is the back of an envelope that I created

for the "Wine of the Month" Club.

Just as with any other form of communication, it's important to test different variables to see what will work best on your envelope.

For one direct mail campaign, I tested two envelopes that I had created for my client, *Ministries Today*. Both versions had a stamp that read "FREE REPORT ENCLOSED: DO NOT BEND." However, each envelope was designed with different tease copy on the outside to get the prospect to open it.

The "Free Report" was designed to get by the gatekeeper, keep it out of the trash, and create curiosity in the pastor who would tear open the envelope.

Envelope A said in large red letters, "A FREE gift for Christian leaders!"

Underneath, in smaller black print it said, "No cost. No obligation. No strings."

Envelope B said in red letters, "Billy Graham ... Jack Hayford ... Tommy Barnett ... Mario Murillo ... David

Yonggi Cho."

Printed on the same places on both envelopes were "FREE Special Report" and "FREE Self-Test Inside."

The majority of people might guess Envelope A, with the word "FREE" at the top won. Wrong. The winner, by 36%, was Envelope B.

By using prominent evangelical leaders that the audience recognized, it created a curiosity about what was inside, much more so than the offer of a FREE gift. This again shows the value of testing.

Letter

The most important component of a traditional direct mail package is a direct response sales letter. To generate the highest number of leads or sales, a letter should be between two and eight pages long. Most lead-generation letters are four pages long.

Some market segments must be longer. The longest letter I've ever created was 16 pages – and it was part of a mailing of more than 2 million pieces, beating the client's control.

The sales letter should include your unique selling proposition (USP), follow a clear and consistent theme, use persuasive direct copy and communicate your valuable offer.

Here are six keys to creating an effective sales letter for your multichannel, integrated marketing campaign:

Key #1: Remember to keep the first sentence short.

Your reader will form an instant impression of your direct mail by reading the first sentence. If it's short and easy to read, chances are better that they'll read on. But if it's slow, long or too complex, they are likely to abandon it.

Key #2: Watch your spacing in the letter.

For the sake of improved readability, single-space the letter and double-space between paragraphs. Most people find this style the easiest to read.

Key #3: Make your intentions clear.

You may tease readers on the outer envelope or subject line, but don't make them read five pages to find out what you're selling. Remember, at the letter's opening you have their attention — so don't be afraid to "fire your biggest gun" at that point.

Key #4: Be believable.

Make sure your principal sales story is feasible. Don't use an episode that's not believable. A prospect respects probability, but will reject something fake.

Key #5: Use a powerful P.S.

Skipping the P.S. is like taking the punch line out of a joke. It just won't work without one.

Perhaps the most effective technique is to throw in a curiosity-building sentence like, "Remember the surprising financial forecast I mentioned on page 2." or "Don't make the #1 mistake I told you about in this letter."

Finally, tell your prospect why he or she must respond right now, and include the phone number or URL. Make them believe that they will miss out on something valuable if they don't act now.

Key #6: Reinforcement is critical.

Check to see if the components of your mailing package reinforce and complement each other. If you have a letter, brochure and lift letter or flyer, don't just repeat the same copy — include references in the letter to "see the brochure for full details." The brochure could include excerpted articles or more benefits.

Remember, an effective sales letter will follow the principles of direct response copy: use the active voice and the word "you," use specifics and stress the benefits of this opportunity to the prospect.

You'll learn more about how to create direct response copy in Chapter 19.

Lift Note

The lift note is a small letter inside the envelope, folded and signed by a credible signer who is not included in the main letter. It's called a "lift note" because it can lift your response by 5–20%. This piece should not be overlooked, and can be a powerful component of your direct response mail package.

The lift note gives a different perspective or reiterates the unique selling proposition (USP) of your offer.

Order Form

The order form is key to the success of a direct mail package because it shows the prospect the way to act on your offer.

One of the primary reasons some direct mail pieces bring in sub-par results is that the response device fails to follow tested and proven direct response rules.

The order form is separate from the letter itself. It can be a variety of sizes, but I recommend 8.5" x 11" or 8.5" x 14" paper.

Here are four elements that your response device must have:

1. A clear call-to-action (CTA). The order form is your chance to clearly describe your offer, guarantee, discount premiums and the most important benefits – all in one spot. Tell your prospects what they will receive by responding to your offer and why they simply cannot wait.

2.   Easy instructions. Prospects must be told exactly how to fill out your order form. If it is not easy to do, they will lose interest and you will lose the sale.

3.   Professional artwork. Remember, your prospect will judge your product or service based on the quality of your response device.

4.   A Positive Acceptance Statement. This powerful copy technique engages the prospect and reinforces how he or she will benefit from your product.

Here's an example for an investment newsletter client:

Strategic Investment Subscription Savings Offer

☑ **Yes, James!** I want exclusive access to your forecasts and recommendations, so I know what's coming … and can make more profitable investments in the months ahead. Please begin my risk-free trial subscription to *Strategic Investment*.

Using the key elements described on the previous pages, you'll be able to create a direct mail package that produces a great response from prospects.

Direct mail packages are great for companies that want to reach the super-wealthy.

Marketing to the Wealthy

Here are two cases of clients I helped to reach wealthy prospects with their offers, target this lucrative market and boost sales significantly.

Morningstar Resort

Morningstar Resort is a country club in Palm Springs, California, that wanted to promote their $1 million+ homes to wealthy prospects, primarily golfers.

They called me to help them increase their leads and conversion while still getting a great ROI.

The best way to do that is with direct response techniques.

Together with my team at Creative Direct Marketing Group, I created an upscale, high-quality, personalized direct mail package that included powerful video and a new approach to list modeling.

The envelope was classy, used the best in personalization and quality. We used "real pen" to create an authentic-looking envelope that prospects would want to rip open.

Their offer was common and boring. So, I beefed it up. Prospects were offered a chance to play a free round of golf at Morningside when they came to look the place over.

And because our list modeling identified the very best prospects, we also offered them the opportunity to spend the night if they chose to do so.

The letter, printed on high-quality paper with a professional-looking gray tint, called the reader's attention to the many benefits of the country club facility, golf course and social connections.

And then we mined the data to create a list for a higher-quality prospect.

This powerful mailer would generate the leads, but what about the conversion?

Our research showed that the spouse often killed the trip and sale, so we emphasized inviting the spouse. In addition, part of the conversion sequence was a powerful video to create a compelling desire for husband and wife to enjoy the experience of visiting.

The results? The million-dollar-homes direct mail piece succeeded in generating quality leads, exceeding all previous offers, and converted the leads into multi-million-dollar sales.

Morningside gained new residents and achieved a higher conversion rate than they had ever experienced.

This was another powerful example of direct mail to deliver quality leads and amazing ROI – producing millions of dollars in profits for Morningstar Resort.

Zacks Money Management

Another client of mine, Zacks Money Management, told me they had a very targeted group of wealthy individuals with whom it was sometimes difficult to communicate.

A broad outreach would not work. As elite money managers, their minimum portfolio was $500 million or more.

So, we developed a 7-point plan to create a marketing campaign that mitigated risk and avoided costly blunders … powerfully boosting sales.

The plan included:

1: Target Audience

For the direct mail campaigns for Zacks, we targeted specifically Accredited Investors with estates of $3 million or more.

#2: Direct Mail Envelope Strategy

When you're dealing with a high-end audience, where people are able to invest more than $500,000, personalization and high quality are essential. That's why we chose to use only the best on the envelope, which looks so authentic that no one can tell it's not personally addressed.

#3: Powerful Direct Mail Letter

For Zacks, we used a powerful two-page letter that also appeared personalized and authentic.

#4: Direct Response Copy

Rather than use editorial or journalistic copy, we used direct response copy. We turned features into benefits and used a strong "you" orientation and highly personal language.

Letters signed by an individual build up credibility and increase response.

#5: A Tactical Lift Note

A lift note can increase response by 10–15%, sometimes as high as 50%. In this case, the lift note used a question: "Your Zacks' #1 rank and 32% return numbers are impressive … but how do they apply to my investment portfolio? See inside."

Readers opened up the short note that had a powerful message. The message had a different theme than the main letter.

#6: A Powerful Order Form

We had a powerful order form with a strong Positive Acceptance Statement (PAS). And the back of it added to the credibility by showing the investment committee team.

#7: A Great Direct Response Offer

The order form included a powerful direct response offer – four bonus reports. We called it the "Safety First Investing Kit." Even the wealthy could not resist the powerful titles that we used, including "How to Protect Your Assets from the Market Downturn or Crash."

Using these seven elements, we produced a powerful direct mail campaign for Zacks that supercharged response from their wealthy target audience.

When created with direct response rules in mind, direct mail can deliver powerful response from prospects. It should be at the core of your lead-generation program ... and your multichannel, integrated approach to a strategic marketing campaign.

I urge you to use this powerful marketing medium. Direct mail is not decreasing in usage or impact. In fact, it's only getting more powerful. Seven in 10 multichannel marketers surveyed said they plan to maintain or increase their use of direct mail through 2019 and beyond.

Traditional direct mail packages are powerful ... but there are additional direct mail formats you can use to effectively market your offer. In addition to this chapter (Chapter 15 - *Traditional Envelope Direct Mail – Little-Known Strategy for Skyrocketing Profits*), chapter 14 and chapter 16 also contribute to direct mail formats you can use to powerfully market your offer.

CHAPTER 16

Magalogs: Infomercials in Print

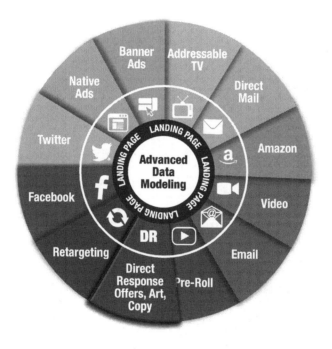

The magalog is a powerful alternative to envelope mailings. It looks and feels like a magazine, but it's actually an "infomercial in print."

The magalog provides a refreshing alternative to the sameness of the traditional direct mail package and has a longer life span and a greater "pass-along" value.

Unlike a traditional catalog, the magalog is not used to sell a variety of products. It focuses on one product or service, with a variety of editorial features that highlight your offer.

This unique direct mail format has produced outstanding results for both consumer and business marketers since I first pioneered the format in the 1990s.

The magalog could be your most effective direct mail choice for your multichannel, integrated marketing campaign. In fact, I recommend it to most of my clients.

Why?

It makes a powerful impression ... communicates the detailed benefits of your offer using an engaging format ... and produces an amazingly positive response.

What does a magalog look like?

When your prospects receive your magalog in the mail, at first they will probably think that it's a regular magazine.

But it's really a detailed sales piece, designed to persuade prospects about the benefits of your offer.

Magalogs are usually 16 pages in length, but they can also be 20, 24, 28 or 32 pages long, since printers find it most convenient to print in sets of four or eight.

Magalogs with page counts in multiples of eight will usually be the least expensive.

In most cases, I recommend 16-20 pages for lead generation and 20–24 pages for selling a product.

Finally, in order to make the magalog look more upscale and reputable, I recommend four-color printing throughout the publication.

Let's look at the key elements for a magalog:

The Cover

The cover of your magalog will have:

- A powerful, direct response graphic
- A bold, persuasive headline
- Informational copy that details what prospects can find inside

A "direct response graphic" might not be the most beautiful image, but it will compel prospects to take action. Usually, this means it looks more "real" than a typical magazine photo.

Take a look at the test below, displaying two different magalog covers I created for Capital Holding Corporation, a life insurance company.

When developing this piece, my mission was to create a cover that the target audience (senior citizens) could relate to.

It was a successful lead generation campaign for reverse mortgages.

Cover A

Cover B

As you can see, Cover A features an elderly woman standing outside her home holding a rake. The copy on the cover was split between both sides of the cover and an additional image (a stack of money) was used to illustrate a headline that read, "Special Focus: A mortgage that pays YOU."

Cover B shows an elderly couple sitting on a chair swing with a cat sitting on the woman's lap. The copy on this cover was lined up in a box to the left and on the bottom in all caps read – "THE GREAT LIFE."

One important thing to note: The woman on Cover A was a real customer of Capital Holding. Underneath her picture in small print down to the right, the copy read: "One Woman's Story: Nikki Grant, Capital Holding customer, Long Beach, California."

Cover B was a professional photograph using models.

Which cover do you think received the higher response?

If you guessed Cover A you're right. Cover A received

an 84% higher response than Cover B. Most marketers guessed cover B because the picture is much better and far more "relational."

But Cover A most likely got the higher response because it's a photo of a real person.

When creating a magalog for your multichannel, integrated campaign, keep this principle in mind: Often, the less professional-looking photo or graphic receives a significantly higher response.

That being said, you should always test different variables to see what works best. The marketplace is always right.

A similar test that I conducted was for a "tabalog" (a variation on the magalog format) that I created for a longtime client, *Health Alert.*

I mailed more than 40 million magalogs, creating the largest alternative health newsletter in America and a $24 million dollar mail order operation.

For one magalog, I tested two different covers: Cover A featured a picture of an elderly man holding his head and looking straight ahead with his eyes open, while Cover B featured an elderly man holding his head but with his face looking down and his eyes shut.

The results showed that Cover B generated a 14.32% better response than Cover A. In this case, Cover B may have gotten a higher response because it evoked more emotion ... but only the marketplace really knows.

Covers should also be informational. Adding page numbers to the story summaries on the cover helps to "tease" the reader inside. See the magalog cover below that I created for my client *Independent Living*, on the next page.

Notice how much copy is included on the cover –

letting prospects know what they can discover inside.

On the bottom, there are short "teaser" snippets from "articles" inside the magalog – showing "see page x" to let readers know exactly where they can find the information.

On some covers, this kind of information is shown as a short list of "teaser bullets." The back cover should also have more statements outlining the articles in the magalog.

Inside the magalog, prospects will find valuable information that describes the benefits of your product or service.

What you say on pages 2 and 3 is critical, and can mean success or failure. Page 2 generally contains a letter from the company president stating the purpose of the magalog, a table of contents or sometimes, the beginning of the lead article.

Page 3 starts the main article.

The lead article helped investor prospects know about a growing energy trend that could help them see skyrocketing profits. This powerful insight was presented in an informational format that the prospect would consider very useful.

In addition to the main articles, prospects will see sidebars throughout the magalog – smaller articles that usually focus on one point or benefit, and then end with a specific reader call-to-action (CTA) to respond.

As with any part of your

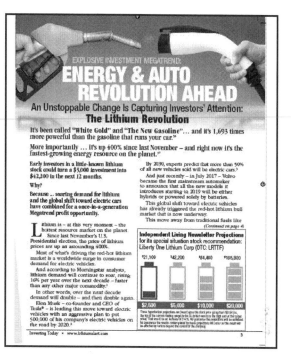

multichannel, integrated marketing campaign, it's critical that you use only direct response copy and art throughout your magalog. You'll discover key rules to this in Chapter 21. Following, not breaking, the rules is critical to your success.

Ultimately, the purpose of this particular magalog was to generate subscribers for an investment newsletter. This is the call-to-action (CTA), presented towards the end of the magalog, along with a response, or order form. The order form is one of the most important components of the magalog, and should take up the last one or two pages.

On the next page, see the two-page order form from the same magalog.

The first page of the order form includes information about the "9 Free Bonuses" that prospects could receive if they subscribed to the newsletter. It also includes a "personal promise" from the newsletter writer that included a guarantee.

The second page of the order form includes a "Positive Acceptance Statement" (PAS) that states exactly what prospects will receive if they respond to the offer:

Yes, Lee! I want to cash in on this explosive energy megatrend and receive early warnings on future megatrends that could have a major impact on my family's financial future. Sign me up immediately for your monthly intelligence advisory, Independent Living. I want to

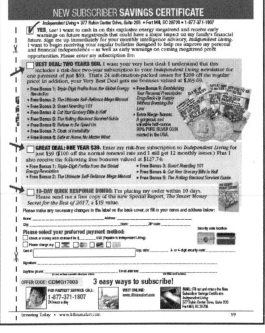

begin receiving your regular bulletins designed to help me improve my personal and financial independence – as well as early warnings on coming megatrend profit opportunities.

Then, it lists different ordering options, as well as a clear, easy-to-understand payment form at the bottom. Prospects are also given options: If they don't want to mail in the form, they can call a toll-free phone number or visit a website.

If your product or service needs more explanation, images, graphs or pictures than can be easily included in a traditional direct mail package, the magalog may be the most effective choice for you.

For example, I often create magalogs for clients who sell financial products or services that may require more details, or for clients who provide financial advice and services.

By offering valuable information – and promising additional, free special reports (which you'll learn more about in Chapter 22) – the magalog helps create trust and interest. Most importantly, it helps generate leads and sales.

Magalogs are valuable, informational and useful … and they produce amazing results.

CHAPTER 17

Unique Direct Mail Formats to Generate Leads and Sales

The Newsalog, Bookalog, Tabalog, Videolog and 3-D Package

The magalog isn't your only direct mail choice for your multichannel, integrated marketing campaign.

Additional unique direct mail formats include:

- 🌐 **The newsalog** – looks like a newspaper … feels like a newspaper … but it's really a marketing piece in disguise

- 🌐 **The bookalog** – a full-length book that offers prospects a powerful value-added piece … and powerful persuasion

- 🌐 **The tabalog** – a stand-out piece that grabs attention from your prospects with its unique size and format

- 🌐 **The videolog** – a unique, high-impact mail format for high-end prospects

- 🌐 **The 3-D package** – a powerful, highly personalized and unique direct mail format that gets a phenomenal response

In the following chapter, you'll discover more about these breakthrough direct mail formats … critical keys to creating effective marketing pieces … and how they can help boost your response.

Newsalogs: Counterintuitive but Effective

Sometimes what's old is new. Newspapers may be in decline, but newsalogs will raise your response rate.

The newsalog is an innovative format that falls in this category of "retromarketing."

I've seen this breakthrough format in direct mail create a 20–30% increase in response for multiple clients.

Like magalogs, newsalogs are really marketing pieces in disguise. They look and feel like an old-fashioned newspaper, but they really drive prospects towards a powerful call-to-action (CTA) to purchase your product or service.

We developed the newsalog when a client came to us looking for a new mailing format. They had tried almost all the traditional mailing formats on their profitable marketing campaigns, including envelope mailings, bookalogs, magalogs and hand-written envelopes.

But multiple mailings to the same names reduce response. This client needed something new to command their prospects' attention and generate new clients.

So, I took the client's old "magalog" or magazine-style format that had been used for various versions for more than 10 years, and turned the copy and art into a mock newspaper.

This advertorial-style format conveyed a sense of newsworthiness about the company and its product, commanded potential customers' attention and, most importantly, dramatically increased our client's sales.

The results?

- A 17% boost response, generating more customers and a superior ROI
- Huge potential for a massive amount of cross-sell revenue

- The most successful year for the company ever, with more than 50,000 new customers added because of the new format

The newsalog is a disruptive format that can "shake things up" if your response rate is stagnant.

Here's an example of a newsalog I created for my client, *Strategic Investment,* an investment newsletter service.

Note the powerful headline: *The End of Chemo* – followed by editorial-style bullet points including: *University of Minnesota Researcher Discovers Breakthrough that Powers Up the Immune System and Destroys Cancer Cells.*

The breaking story that followed described a powerful new innovation in cancer treatment that could remove the need for chemotherapy, radiation and surgery.

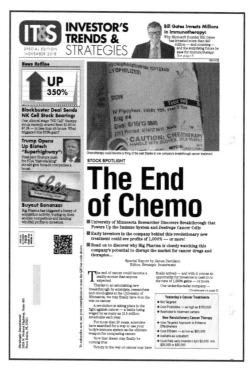

In reality, the story is meant to persuade readers to want to invest in the company behind this cancer breakthrough – a powerful investment opportunity presented by my client's investment newsletter, *Strategic Investment.*

Inside the newsalog, prospects find additional articles as well as detailed stock projections for the company behind the cancer treatment.

Like magalogs, newsalogs contain a detailed order form and call-to-action at the end of the direct mail format. Newsalogs look and feel authentic, using the same paper type, size and color as a traditional newspaper.

Here are three foundational principles that apply to newsalogs:

1. Newsalogs are typically 20–28 pages in length; 20–24 for leads, 20–28 for sales.

2. Newsalogs are written in a more editorial style, but still follow the principles of direct response copy – benefit-oriented, "you-focused" copy.

3. Newsalogs also use direct response art and graphics to generate a high response from the reader.

Newsalogs may be an especially effective choice for you if you sell a more complicated service or product that requires more explanation.

Here is the winning newsalog control that beat all formats and over 12 covers for *Health Alert*.

Bookalogs: A High-Impact Lead Generation Tool

While Bookalogs aren't brand-new to direct mail formats, they are frequently overlooked or rarely chosen in the marketing world. But, Bookalogs are easily amongst the most compelling marketing pieces you can offer, therefore they should invariably be considered.

In politics, every serious candidate has one.

That's because a bookalog acts as a powerful branding and positioning piece by establishing you as an "expert" or "authority" in your space.

And one of the great advantages of the bookalog is that it provides you with an opportunity to build credibility in the eyes of your prospect – and set you apart in a very powerful way from the competition.

People respect books ... and they also respect authors.

A bookalog is excellent for either business-to-business or consumer campaigns. It's also shown to be a successful tool for fundraising, investment offers, health offers, tech campaigns and much more.

Though a bookalog is an effective marketing vehicle,

it is not viewed as a sales piece. Rather, it is considered a book, with valuable information to be learned, acted on and shared with others.

Here's an example of a bookalog I created for a client generating leads for a financial service ... along with the envelope it came in.

The title of the book was *6 Blunders That Could Destroy Your Retirement Dreams!*

The subtitle said, "How you can avoid common investment mistakes that can turn your golden years into a nightmare."

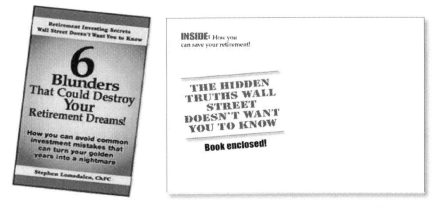

This book was a sales piece written for my client's "perfect prospects" – using highly targeted mailing lists. Prospects were not being "sold," but educated. The goal: by the time recipients put down the "book," they had learned a lot. Yet, in reality, the bookalog had one basic and specific objective, and that was to generate leads from prospects who enjoyed the information or story presented in the book.

Most bookalogs I create are about 120 pages, softbound and have all the features of a normal book (i.e., a table of contents, a dedication and an appealing title that makes the recipient want to read it).

Usually we also create a hard cover version for special prospects.

Here are eight rules to keep in mind when creating your bookalog:

1. Your copy needs to follow the time-tested, direct response rules for copy. Remember, it's a sales piece, not an editorial (See Chapter 19).

2. Use an easy-to-read typeface that is 12-point or above.

3. Choose your author wisely. Typically, the author would be your company president, but it depends on the product or service. A physician is a great choice for a nutritional product, for example, while a teacher makes a great spokesperson for an educational program.

4. For a powerful direct mailing campaign that complements your multichannel, integrated campaign, include a simple, one-page letter in an envelope along with the bookalog. Use the letter to explain why the prospect has received the book, what's in it for them and why they need to read it.

5. You must include an order form that is separate from your direct mail sales letter and the book. Print several order forms at the end of the bookalog itself. If the book is passed around, this ensures each reader will have a chance to respond to your offer. Use the same order form techniques that are key to every other direct mail piece.

6. Create an e-book version of your book that you can use for digital components of your multichannel, integrated campaign. And yes, put it on Amazon.

7. Print both hard-cover copies and soft-cover copies. Soft-cover books can be used for general

distribution. The hard-cover can be used for personal distribution at important meetings. Nothing is more powerful than signing the book for a prospect or client – you're the author!

8. Finally, testing your bookalog is crucial and can be accomplished in a variety of ways. As with a direct mail letter, the results will depend on using the right mailing list, superior direct response copy, creative direction of the book and the right offer to generate a lead from the potential customer.

If you want to create powerful credibility, position yourself as an expert in your field and set yourself apart from 98% of marketers who have never even considered using a book. Do it skillfully and a bookalog might be an effective choice for your direct mail campaign.

The Tabalog: A Rare Marketing Format That Breaks Through the Clutter

Even rarer than the bookalog is the tabalog, a direct mail marketing piece that makes a powerful impression on prospects because of its unusual size and format.

The tabalog looks similar to a magazine, except that it is enlarged from typical magazine dimensions to 11" x 12". When I create a tabalog, I use a coated stock cover to create extra impact.

Here's a powerful story about how we created a tabalog to supercharge response for an alternative health client:

My client Sun Wellness wanted to aggressively expand its customer base for its Sun Chlorella supplement. For about four years, the company had been mailing a traditional envelope mailing package I created to grow its market share. But Sun Wellness wanted to speed up its progress. The marketplace was becoming increasingly competitive as many new nutraceutical companies were entering the market, and the company's target prospects were being inundated with advertising.

My job was to help Sun Chlorella stand out among the crowd – and generate more leads and profits.

So, I decided to use a tabalog to create interest and curiosity, and capture the attention of prospects who would turn into loyal customers.

The primary function of Sun Chlorella was to help the body cleanse and detoxify itself naturally. To highlight this, my team and I developed a tabalog around the theme of "the invisible toxic enemy."

The cover featured the true story of Dr. William Kellas, a noted authority on toxins and the immune system, and his own path from a debilitating disease to better health using the 7-Step "Health & Vitality" program. Developed around Sun Chlorella, the program was highlighted throughout the piece, and was supported by health facts, expert opinions and customer testimonials.

The campaign's special offer included a 30% discount and up to four Free Bonus gifts.

The results?

Campaign performance was three times greater than the company's previous mailing.

This tabalog mailing not only helped Sun Wellness expand their customer base, but they had to expand their staff and install a new phone system to keep up with the number of orders that were coming in. More than 4 million pieces were mailed, which generated thousands of new buyers.

This powerful story demonstrates how a unique direct

mail piece, such as the tabalog (but even the bookalog or newsalog) can help response to your multichannel, integrated campaign skyrocket.

The Videolog: A High-End Piece for High-End Prospects

You may have a product or service offer that you would like to send to a select group of high-end prospects.

Maybe you're willing to spend more cash upfront to make an immediate, powerful impression and get an amazingly positive response.

If that's the case, you should definitely consider using a videolog to market your product or service to a select audience.

A videolog is one of the newest technological advancements in direct response marketing. It is a specially designed device included in a mailing that automatically plays a video when opened by the prospect. A screen is included on the device itself, which is opened by the recipient like a brochure.

Videologs command attention … and invite response.

They are stunning pieces that have probably never been seen by your prospects before.

The video itself can be two minutes, three minutes or even 30 minutes. And it can feature a large or small screen. It can even include a button to make a phone call on the spot to respond to your offer, without ever touching a cell phone.

For the videolog, I create a powerful direct response video with the proper copy, as explained in Chapter

27. It's delivered in an envelope with a cover letter, a small brochure that has the video and a lift note. The impact is spectacular!

The latest version includes a phone built in so all your prospects have to do is push a button to generate the lead or sale.

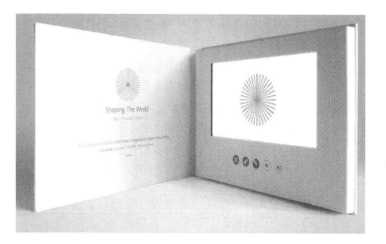

Videologs will be your priciest option for your direct mail package – but they also get an outstanding average response of 14% or higher.

I expect that the cost of creating a videolog will decrease in the near future ... allowing you to create a high-impact piece at a relatively low cost ... with a low cost-per-lead and cost-per-sale.

The 3-D Package: Generating Leads with a Creative, High-Impact Piece

A 3-D package is a high-impact piece that uses a creatively oversized or odd-sized package that has the enticing appearance of a gift.

These packages are usually sent via Federal Express or UPS and are designed to get past the mailroom (if mailed to an office) and into the hands of the targeted decision maker, grabbing their full attention.

3-D packages get an extraordinary response because of their unique format. Even the most jaded direct mail recipient will find it difficult to resist opening a mysterious package that looks like a gift.

The package might be an odd-sized envelope, a cardboard or wooden box or a tube. The contents could be a jigsaw puzzle with missing pieces, the beginning of a collection of special items, a lock with an offer to deliver the key — or a variety of other items that come from an especially creative imagination.

If you are trying to market your product or service to a highly targeted audience, this is one of the most effective ways to get your message to the right people with the greatest immediate impact and the highest possible response rate.

These intrusive hands-on pieces usually trigger a response rate that is five to 50 times the normal rate of a traditional mailing piece.

3-D packages are more costly than traditional direct mail – easily $10 to $75 per piece. So, they should be reserved for high-margin products or services and are usually sent to target audiences of about 10,000 or fewer.

Here are the details of a 3-D campaign I created for a client:

The prospect was given a pair of scissors and a coupon to "cut their shipping costs in half." The campaign on the right featured a 1-dollar bill and a 2-dollar bill. It

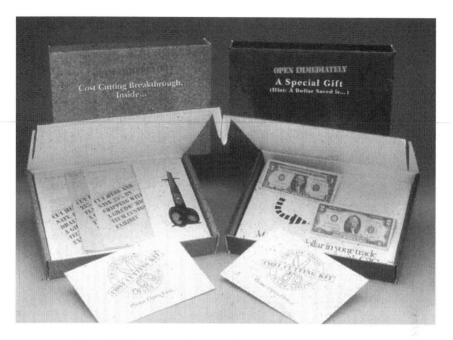

was a visual play on how the prospect could double his or her money.

As you can see, a three-dimensional campaign is a mailer that shows a concept or a theme in a clever, interesting way. It's also highly memorable – and fun for your prospect.

This package also contained a sales letter and a lift note to tell the story. I recommend you include these traditional components in your piece as well as newer items.

Both pieces received more than a 20% response rate – and increased even more by follow-up phone calls.

With a 3-D campaign, you're able to break through the clutter, make your presentation dramatic and interesting and set the stage for your phone contact or sales call. If the prospect doesn't call first, a good salesperson will initiate a call with the reminder: "We're the company that sent you the...." It's amazing how creative three-dimensional packages break down barriers.

These formats often seem counterintuitive or even overly "retro" – but the proof is in the amazing results: Your prospects will respond to a unique direct mail format, especially when it is carefully created with direct response principles and tactics.

And, when integrated into your multichannel, integrated marketing campaign, these pieces will help you achieve a tremendous response – and produce profits that will make you come back for more!

CHAPTER 18

Informed Delivery – The "Pre-Mail" Alert

"Informed Delivery" is a cutting-edge new marketing tool that you can use with your direct mail.

It's a special email that alerts your direct mail recipients that the direct mail piece will arrive that very day in their postal mailbox.

It reinforces your offer...

Provides another touchpoint...

And increases your response...

And it's FREE!

That's because Informed Delivery is provided by the U.S. Postal Service.

The Postal Service provides Informed Delivery at no cost to anyone who signs up. The program allows you to:

1) Display an image of your envelope in the email that announces what's coming that day to a recipient's mailbox, and

2) Include a banner ad below the image of your direct mail piece.

And you can use it for your multichannel, integrated marketing campaign – to boost your response and reinforce your offer.

What Will You Get in the Mail Today?

People love looking at this email. It's addictive. It's a sneak preview. The email shows all the mail coming that day with a photo image offering more. If you get one piece in your mailbox, it shows it. If you get 20, it shows you all 20.

That means that when you send your prospects a powerful direct mail piece – either a traditional mailing package or another type of format detailed in this book – they will receive an email displaying your direct mail package before they receive it in their postal mailbox.

The USPS sends this email for you … but you can still customize it with a link to your landing page or video.

Take a look at the example of what "Informed Delivery" looked like for my client *Independent Living*, an investment newsletter:

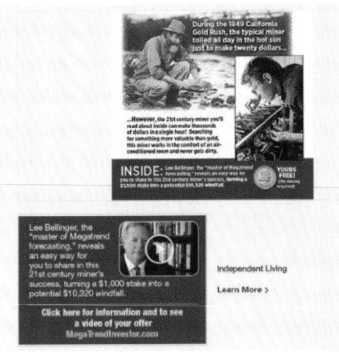

In this case, prospects can see what the incoming direct mail magalog looks like. It's creating curiosity and anticipation.

Below the magalog image, we showed a tease of the landing page.

Prospects then have the opportunity to immediately visit the landing page and respond to the offer.

Informed delivery will also allow you to run a free banner ad that drives prospects to a video.

Here is an example:

Informed delivery gives you a powerful opportunity to enhance your direct mail campaign – and your multichannel, integrated marketing campaign – and should be used in every direct mail campaign you conduct.

Part Four

Multichannel, Integrated Creative Essentials to Maximizing Response

You might have all of the assets in place for a multichannel, integrated marketing campaign...

But if your assets aren't created with the right creative approach, your marketing simply won't succeed.

In the following five chapters (Chapters 19–23), you'll discover time-tested, proven strategies to producing creative content that gets a response.

CHAPTER 19

Writing Copy That Sells

50 Rules for Creating Effective, Sales-Boosting Copy

In the previous 18 chapters, we took a look at the individual elements that make up your multichannel, integrated marketing campaign.

Now, let's dive into one of the core foundations that will make your multichannel, integrated campaign effective and profitable: direct response copy.

You may create and deploy all elements of a successful marketing campaign … but get a very low return on your blood, sweat and tears if the content of your campaign copy falls flat.

The hallmarks of effective marketing are not beautiful aesthetics and clever writing. Effective marketing is never measured by what seems to look or sound good. It's measured by its rate of success.

Here's the bottom line: Effective marketing will motivate your prospect to pick up the phone and call your toll-free number – or go to your website and enter a credit card number.

So, what's going to drive your prospects to respond to your offer?

The Foundation of Successful Marketing: Direct Response Copywriting

More than beautiful graphics or short, cute copy, direct response copywriting will motivate your prospects to purchase your product or service.

Direct response copy is a unique, conversational style of copy that turns features into benefits. It develops credibility and reality in your advertising campaign.

In short: It's persuasive "word engineering" that gets people to respond.

In more than 40 years of writing direct response marketing materials, I have developed some critical foundations of direct response copywriting that should always be followed for increased response. These include a set of powerful foundations, tried-and-true formulas for writing great copy and direct response rules that should never be broken.

These time-tested strategies and tactics should be applied to every aspect of your integrated marketing campaign: landing page, direct mail, email, banner ads, Facebook ads, pre-roll video, email and more.

Direct response copy succeeds because it's based in science

Most advertising agencies create art: beautiful design with clever copy. But if you want to get new leads and customers, attractive art is only a small part of the battle.

Direct response marketing is based on the science of what makes advertising effective and why. Using tried-and-true rules, direct response copy will:

- Grab the attention of your prospect.
- Powerfully position your company and product in your prospect's mind.
- Identify your unique selling proposition (USP).
- Overcome your prospect's skepticism and objections.

- Create a "branding" effect that will help you gain market share.
- Motivate your prospect to respond immediately.
- Follow time-tested copy rules that work.

Direct response copy begins with you.

Direct response copy doesn't necessarily begin with a clever idea. It begins with "you."

A good direct response copywriter will:

- Discover what's unique about your product or service and relate it to the "you" orientation of the prospect.

- Decide exactly how your prospects will benefit from your product or service.

- Create a specific, clear theme for the prospect.

- Develop personal, one-on-one communication with the prospect.

- Communicate your unique selling proposition (USP) to your prospect – what sets apart your product or service from the rest (see Chapter 20).

Good direct response copy draws on the core emotional needs of your prospect. The desire for money, love, respect and self-improvement are some of the strongest emotions you can appeal to. Show your prospects how your product or service will meet those needs, and they'll find your offer irresistible.

Direct response copy focuses on one "Big Idea."

A good direct response copywriter will focus on one big idea: a single, strong theme that can be explained clearly and understood quickly. A big idea lets your prospect know right away what you're getting at.

The best "big ideas" are closely tied to your audience's strongest trigger points. They're timely and emotionally stirring, to awaken, shock or fascinate your reader. They work because they make a strong connection with your reader.

If you can't describe your big idea in just a few words … then you don't have one.

Revisit your approach and search for that one idea that will reach the real needs, fears and concerns of your prospect.

If you use direct response strategies effectively, your prospects will clearly understand how your offer meets their needs and desires. Your prospects become your customers because they see what's in it for them if they buy from you.

Direct response copy stresses the benefits, not the features, of your product or service.

Traditional advertising copy will tell you about the features of a product or service. For example, an ad for a stroller might tell you that it's "lightweight," has "all-terrain wheels" or features an "adjustable handlebar."

By contrast, direct response copy will tell you about the benefits of a product or service. For example, it might describe a stroller as "convenient to carry," "ideal for the outdoors" and "simple to use for both parents."

Do you see the difference?

Features pertain to the product or service. Benefits tell the buyers what the features do for them. Here are three simple rules for telling your prospects about the benefits of your product or service – and getting more sales.

Rule #1: Decide exactly how your buyers will benefit from the most important features of your product or service ... and tell them how these features benefit them.

If you are selling an extremely compact pocket knife, your benefit could be: "slips into your pocket easily because it's so tiny."

If you are selling a high-quality set of precision golf clubs, your benefit could be "highest precision and extreme accuracy help you lower your score."

Rule #2: Determine your prospects' exact needs and desires ... so you can give them the right kind of compelling copy that makes them want to buy from you.

Figure out precisely: What do your buyers want? What are their goals? What makes them most happy?

For example, with a less expensive, more powerful vacuum cleaner the "you" method produces the benefit, "you can save with our low prices."

Rule #3: Put yourself in your buyer's shoes before you write one word of copy.

Just imagine that someone else is trying to sell your product or service to you.

What benefits should they mention to convince you to buy it?

What order should these benefits be in? How should they be presented for the most successful sales story?

What strongest benefit should be the "clincher" that

closes the sale?

Use the valuable information you glean by imagining that someone else is trying to sell your product or service to you ... and put all this information into strong selling copy!

Long copy almost always works better than short copy.

It might seem counterintuitive, but extensive research and testing have shown that long copy almost always works better than short copy.

A long letter in a direct mail piece, a long email or text-heavy landing page will usually generate a higher response from your prospective customers. Readership does fall off at 300 words, but does not drop off again until 3,000 words.

Take a look at the five-way test, shown below. This test was conducted to compare results using several different sizes of brochures, sales letters and a self-mailer.

This five-way test clearly demonstrates two important

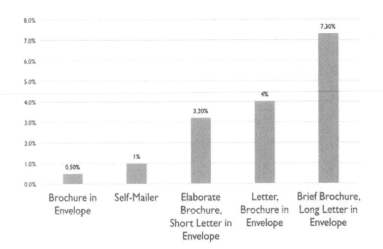

facts.

The first is that a letter is one of the most important marketing materials you can invest in.

The second important fact? As you can see from the test results, response to a long letter can significantly outpull response to a short letter.

Generating high-quality leads requires copy that is long enough to properly tell your story to a skeptical audience.

Your marketing deserves a sales letter, landing page, video and other media that:

🌍 Pack an emotional wallop.

🌍 Show your prospects what's unique about you.

🌍 Explain why your offer will benefit them more than competitors' offers.

🌍 Overcome their hesitation and objections.

Involving your readers and telling them exactly what you want them to do might take more than one or two pages of copy.

Lead copy should be shorter than sales copy that's asking for a sale. Also, the more you're asking for – especially $5,000 or more – or the more complicated your opportunity is to understand, the longer the copy needs to be.

Direct response copy is a better return on your investment.

For decades, direct marketers using direct response copy have:

- Compiled the response rate to tens of

thousands of emails, web ads, paid search, direct mail packages, radio spots and television commercials…

- Compared marketing copy and strategies with the quantity and quality of responses…

- Discovered which strategies and tactics were hugely successful, which were moderately successful and which were devastating failures…

- Analyzed exactly why successful marketing strategies and techniques earned their companies millions of dollars and why some didn't…

- And validated their discoveries through solid measurement and analysis, testing and more testing.

Over the years, I have developed a knowledge base of copy strategies and techniques that work, as well as when they work and why, which I'll share with you on the following pages.

Writing great copy requires mastery of direct marketing strategies and techniques.

An image-based advertising agency wants you to believe that no one can write sales copy like their clever copywriters. Don't believe them.

Even great writers don't necessarily write great copy. More than perfect prose or even perfect grammar, powerful direct response copy will convince a prospect to respond to your offer.

Tried-and-True Formulas to Create Effective Copy for Your Multichannel, Integrated Campaign

Here are four formulas to help you succeed in creating persuasive, powerful direct response copy that will boost your sales.

The 4 "P's"

The 4 "P's" is a basic copy formula to keep in mind while making sure you've included all of the core elements of effective direct response copy.

The 4 "P's" include:

- **Promise.** Catch your readers' attention by promising them a benefit. Call it out in the headline, elaborate on it in the subhead and then expand further in your opening. Showing your readers what's in it for them is the only surefire way to grab attention.

- **Picture.** Help your readers imagine themselves enjoying the benefit or outcome you've promised. This approach appeals to your prospects' emotional triggers. Specifically elaborate on how your product or service will make this benefit a reality.

- **Proof.** Back up the picture you've painted with cold, hard facts: Statistics, research studies, charts, graphs, testimonials, third-party reviews, certifications, product photos and product demonstrations.

- **Push.** This is more than just a call to action — it's also delivering your irresistible offer and illustrating how much value your recipient will receive. Your goal is to link the promised benefit to the enticing picture to the acceptance of the proof ... all to result in an action.

The 5 "U's"

The 5 "U's" are a simple code for creating copy that is compelling, interesting and effective. Consider what your 5 "U's" will be before you write your copy.

The 5 "U's" are:

1. **Unusual approach.** Every day, your prospects see dozens, if not hundreds of messages in their postal mail, email, Facebook feeds, in pre-roll videos and more. If you want to get noticed, do something different. Try a powerful headline that speaks directly to your target. Highlight an unusual, but strong offer. Or provide a guarantee that stands out from the rest.

2. **Urgent feel.** Unless you can convince your customers to take immediate action, you're at risk of losing them forever. To convey a sense of urgency, give the product or service you're offering a limited window of time in which to buy. Also, be sure to offer valid reasons for the urgency, not just an arbitrary deadline.

3. **Useful and valuable information.** Your email, Facebook ads, pre-roll commercials or direct mail letters should include some intrinsic value. Offering real value to your audience will greatly increase response.

4. **Unique Selling Proposition (USP).** What makes you special? Why should a customer buy from

you instead of your competitor? How is your offer better than anything else on the market? Your USP differentiates you in such a way as to make you the most compelling choice for your customers.

5. Ultra-specific and details. Test after test prove it … specifics outsell generalities every time. Use specific numbers (tests show that odd numbers do better than even). Provide facts supported by percentages. Use names of authoritative figures when appropriate. Avoid vague copy and provide details that sell.

AIDA: Attention, Interest, Desire, Action

AIDA works because it keeps you focused on the final goal: Prompting your reader to act. Use AIDA as the "line of action" as you write your copy.

First, grab your prospect's attention with a personal, benefit-driven headline.

Now that you've got their attention, what you say next is critical. You must create interest to keep them reading. Help them quickly identify that your message is relevant.

To build desire, use your strongest benefit-driven selling points to appeal to your prospects' needs and wants.

Finally, get your prospects to take action by clearly stating what you want them to do. For example, "Call 1-800-XXX-XXXX to get your free recession-fighting report" or "Return this Special Savings Certificate in the postage-paid envelope today to begin your FREE, no-risk, 30-day trial."

AIDPPC: Attention, Interest, Description, Persuasion, Proof, Close

AIDPPC is a variation on AIDA that provides a winning formula to get prospects to take action.

After you've got their attention and interest, your curious prospects will want a full description of what you're offering. Show your readers how your offer will improve their lives by describing the benefits of your product or service.

And remember, persuasion goes beyond simply presenting interesting information. You must convince prospects that it's in their best interest to respond to your offer.

After you've made your claims, provide proof. Today's skeptical prospects demand that you prove your statements. Back up your sales pitch with cold, hard facts and testimonials.

Finally, close. Summarize the benefits and the offer, and pair them with your call to action.

These copy formulas provide a good foundation for writing an effective direct response piece.

In addition, you must also know specific direct response copy rules. After all, direct response marketing is persuasive word engineering that relies on a set of foundational rules.

Over the years, I've worked on thousands of ads, direct mail pieces, landing pages, emails and more. And from all of this work, it's clear that certain types of copy are most successful.

These are words, phrases and sentence types that can be tested for effectiveness.

Simply put, experience has shown that this is the kind of copy that works best.

I've found that you can produce the best copy by following a set of rules. Break the rules and bad things happen.

50 Rules for Direct Response Copy

Here are 50 rules for direct response copy that I use for every element of an effective multichannel, integrated marketing campaign.

Keep these principles in mind during all of your marketing efforts – direct mail, email, TV commercials, your landing page, video script, banner ads and everything else you use – and you'll see great response.

Rule #1 Remember to keep the first sentence short.

Your reader will form an instant impression of your offer by reading the first sentence. If it's short and easy to read, chances are better that he or she will read on. But if it's slow, long or too complex, the reader is more likely to abandon it.

Rule #2 Make sure your intentions are clear.

You may tease a reader on the outer envelope or headline of your landing page, but don't make your prospect read five pages to find out what you're selling. As a marketer, you're competing with multiple distractions that hinder your ability to drive a sale.

Remember, you have their attention at the opening – so don't be afraid to "fire your biggest gun" at that point.

Here's an example of a strong opening:

I'm going to tell you about a natural health product that heals your aches and pains just as well as prescription medications – but with no side effects whatsoever. Not even one.

Or:

Dozens of online investment newsletters promise great stock tips. But my service does more than promise great tips. It also teaches you the 18 foolproof criteria for identifying great stocks...so you can become your own high-powered Wall Street advisor.

Rule #3 Approach the reader from a position of authority.

The feel of the copy, the tone, the energy – must come across as authoritative. Authoritative copy means words that include specific information, details, figures and facts that will resonate.

Your readers must feel confident that the copy is speaking to them with authority and conviction. Your copy must relate to their challenges and solve their concerns.

Rule #4 Use specifics to strengthen your copy.

Don't just write that your product or service is unique. Tell the reader why, and use concrete examples.

Rule #5 Use specifics in your testimonials.

For a health supplement, don't use, "Your vitamin is terrific. I feel great." Instead use, "I tried your vitamin... so far, I feel more energetic and focused. I'm sleeping better and I feel less anxious." Give your readers "meat," not generalizations.

Rule #6 Make sure what you provide is exciting to the reader.

Sometimes what's exciting and important to you isn't interesting to the prospect. So, you need to understand and key in on his or her needs and concerns, not yours.

Rule #7 Avoid the passive voice.

Isolate and review all phrases telling what you'll do for the person. Then make sure to change a passive voice to an active voice. Don't write, "The kit will be forwarded to you immediately." Instead, simply write, "I'll send you your kit now."

Rule #8 Use the word "now."

To stress immediacy, use the word "now" to persuade prospects to act immediately. Your best opportunity to make a sale is immediately – before something or someone else grabs their attention.

Rule #9 Remember that benefits outsell descriptions.

Increasing "you-benefit" copy and minimizing mechanical descriptions mean better response. You won't sell a car by describing the type of safety glass or the gauge of steel, but a buyer will respond if you emphasize benefits: great handling, increased gas mileage, high resale value, performance, etc.

Rule #10 Zero in on reader action.

Your objective is to make the prospect say, "Yes, I'll buy!" If he or she doesn't act positively, then the only thing you've succeeded in doing is keeping your name alive as a reminder. Give readers the answers to their questions. Don't keep them guessing.

Also, don't forget to get the reader's head nodding

in agreement. Keep him or her reading by maintaining the "yes" mood.

Rule #11 Write sentences so they're short and easy to read.

Instead of saying, "You can buy this product now," say, "Buy now."

Rule #12 Avoid big words when shorter words are available.

"Buy" instead of "purchase." "Get" instead of "receive." "Need" instead of "require."

Rule #13 Cut long paragraphs into several short ones.

Short paragraphs are easier to skim and read quickly. Try to keep your paragraphs to one or two sentences – three, maximum.

Rule #14 Indent and use white space to its advantage.

Your prospect shouldn't be overwhelmed by words packed onto a page. You're not writing a textbook. Leave white space on the page. It has a powerful effect.

Rule #15 Select hot words.

…such as "new," "now," "easy," "introducing" and "save." These are the words that will capture the attention of your prospects and get them to respond.

Rule #16 Vary paragraph lengths.

Keep paragraphs short – as stated in Rule #13 – but make sure they aren't all the same length. Some paragraphs should be one short sentence. Others might be two longer sentences.

Again, none of your paragraphs should be extremely long.

Rule #17 Make sentences and paragraphs flow with natural transitions.

Use transitional words and phrases to flow from one idea to the next. For example, you can say "Let me tell you…" or "Next,"

Rule #18 Occasionally insert a paragraph that has just a word or two, or a single sentence.

Don't be afraid of using just one or two words on one line, or one short sentence. This helps keep your copy conversational and engaging.

Rule #19 Use color for subheads, bullets and indentations.

Rule #20 Present information in easy-to-understand charts and graphs.

In today's fast-paced, low-attention-span environment, simple, visual displays of information are very effective.

That's why it's especially important to reinforce your copy (specifically comparisons, ratios and percentages) with a chart or graph that visually represents your content.

And make sure you always write a descriptive caption explaining exactly what the reader is looking at.

Rule #21 Avoid bureaucratic talk. Never assume they all know the lingo.

Rule #22 Don't choose odd words that will pull readers' attention away from the sales message.

Rule #23 Weed out clichés and jargon.

Rule #24 Avoid too many commas and semicolons.

They'll slow your readers down.

Rule #25 Your headline should contain a benefit.

Start your ad, brochure, webpage, email or any other marketing tool off with a bang ... meaning put your biggest benefit right in the headline.

Use your headline to grab your prospects' attention immediately, so they will quickly understand that the message is meant for them.

Rule #26 Never ask a question in a headline.

Question marks in a headline depress response. They cancel out any prospect who would answer the question with "No."

There are exceptions, but they are rare. If the question creates shock, it may be effective. But think carefully about the risk.

Rule #27 Steer clear of new language.

Slang words and phrases may jar, offend or confuse readers with meanings they may not know.

Rule #28 Omit words that convey doubt or uncertainty:

"I think," "It appears," "It seems," "You might find."

Rule #29 Write in a language that's "you," not "I" oriented.

- "You'll gain" (not "I provide")
- "You'll discover" (not "I'll show you")
- "You'll get a free" (not "I'll give you")

Rule #30 Write in an active voice.

"You'll get your free book," not "The free book will be forwarded to you."

Rule #31 Use the present tense:

"Buy now and you'll get a free bonus."

Rule #32 Write to one person, from one person.

Rule #33 Write your copy "out loud."

To ensure your copy is conversational, take the time to read it out loud.

It should sound like a real face-to-face conversation.

Rule #34 Don't brag – let the facts brag for you.

Rule #35 Don't say "trust me."

Here's the problem: Your prospects aren't going to trust you just because you tell them to. You actually have to earn that trust.

When you say to your prospect, "You can trust me," without backing that up with certifiable proof, you sound exactly like the con artists you're trying to distinguish yourself from.

Focus on proving your claims with real, hard-hitting testimonials. If you can do all that, you'll win their trust – and their business.

Rule #36 Pepper copy with proven power words.

Power words alert your prospects and grab their attention. Instead of announcing or describing the product like hot words do, power words are packed with action.

Here are 10 power words to use in your next campaign:

1. Own
2. Get
3. Control
4. Take
5. Capture
6. Try
7. Enjoy

8. Seize

9. Grab

10. Have

Rule #37 Use exclamation points, but sparingly!

Sometimes you do need to punctuate your excitement. But be careful not to go overboard. Too many exclamation points make your copy sound cheesy or even worse – unbelievable. But in other cases, they are needed to change the tone.

See how differently these examples read, thanks to punctuation:

Wrong: Easy to understand. You even get email contacts.

Right: Easy to understand. You even get email contacts!

Wrong: Revealed: The secret to a crash-proof portfolio!

Right: Revealed: The secret to a crash-proof portfolio.

If you're not sure, consider your audience and your product. Products that are serious in nature, as well as luxury items, will rarely use exclamation points in print advertising.

Rule #38 Don't use asterisks (*).

Rule #39 Use ellipses (. . .) instead of dashes (–).

Rule #40 Avoid exaggerated claims.

They will destroy your credibility. Superlatives are counterproductive. To claim that your service or product is the best in the world is automatically ignored by the reader and casts doubt on your entire presentation.

On the other hand, when you are specific and use actual testimonials, you gain credibility. Let others verify your facts and greatness, and let details and specifics reinforce your claims.

Rule #41 Avoid complicated words.

Simple words are powerful words. Legendary copywriter John Caples once said, "The headline of an ad for an automobile repair kit was, 'How to repair cars.' The headline was changed to, 'How to fix cars.' The second headline pulled 20% more replies."

Rule #42 Anticipate the beliefs of your prospects.

Don't try to change the beliefs and attitudes of your prospects – track with them.

Do your research on your prospects. Speak to their political beliefs and their worldview, and they'll be more likely to respond to your offer.

Rule #43 Eliminate all references to "I think" or "our company believes."

Remember, your prospects don't care about what you think, they only care about what they think or need.

Rule #44 Anticipate and address your prospect's questions.

Write your copy as if you were face to face with your prospects and anticipating their questions.

Rule #45 Anticipate and respond to your prospect's objections.

An objection is often a question. One way to turn a potential negative into an advantage is with a question-and-answer format.

Rule #46 Write a list.

Writing a list will help readers who simply "skim" your copy pick up on your points quickly and read through to your call-to-action.

Rule #47 Relate your product or service to items in the news.

Be careful to make sure that the news item is timely

and relevant to your product and its benefits.

Rule #48 Define your unique selling proposition (USP).

Do it at the start and reinforce it in the middle and at the end. This is what sets you apart — make sure it weaves through your entire message. You'll learn more about how to define your USP in Chapter 20.

Rule #49 Position your company as an authority with a solution to your target's worst problem.

Make it clear that you are the obvious and best resource to meet your prospect's needs. Speak with authority, and your prospects will trust you to help solve their problems.

Rule #50 Choose only direct response copy in all of your marketing materials.

Finally, use only direct response copy in your multichannel, integrated marketing campaign. Don't be tempted to deviate! Your materials should all work together, relying on powerful, direct response principles to drive a sale.

Now that you know the rules of direct response copywriting, let's take a look at a few pieces that show you how it works in action...

4 Examples of Direct Response Copy That Got Real Response

In more than 40 years of marketing, I have seen the power of direct response copy work again and again to get a high response, generate new leads and produce millions of dollars in profits for my clients.

Below, you'll find four examples of direct response

copy used in pieces that got great response ... and helped my clients powerfully expand their businesses.

Envelope Copy for Monaco Rare Coins

"The U.S. government had most of these coins melted down in the 1930s ... but a handful escaped into European vaults ... and they're now available to you."

This intriguing detail directly addresses prospects and tells them what they can get ... and why it's unique and valuable.

Sales Letter for Wine of the Month Club

"Imagine the rare pleasure of savoring exceptional new wines every month.

Wines handpicked for you by the world's leading wine experts. Wines you'll rarely find on the store shelves in club warehouses."

Again, note the "you"-orientation in this copy, and focus on how this client's subscription service would enhance the lives of readers with rare, exceptional wines.

Magalog Order Form for Independent Living Investment Newsletter

"Secure Your Access to Early Megatrend Warnings – and the Blockbuster Profit Opportunities That Follow!"

This exciting call-to-action uses power words like "megatrend" and "blockbuster" ... and stays in the present tense.

Retargeting Banner Ad for World Opportunity Investor

"Video explains it all. Did you see it?"

This retargeting ad uses short sentences and "you-orientation" to instantly create a two-way dialogue with prospects.

Of course, there are tens of thousands of examples I

could show you … all of which follow a set of careful guidelines to generate response.

A Final Step: Capture the Attention of "Skimmers" with Your Copy

A "skimmer" is a reader who won't read through your copy carefully. Instead, they'll simply "skim" your copy to pick up what's important and relevant.

Here are three direct response strategies to capture the attention of "skimmers":

1. **Write powerful headlines and sub-headlines.** A long headline with specific details can pull in otherwise reluctant readers. Use words like "shocking," "secret" and "finally."

2. **Use captions.** Skimmers may not read the bulk of your body copy, but they will read captions. Write captions for all of your images, graphics and photos.

3. **Include pull quotes.** A pull quote is a portion of text that "pops out" from the rest of the copy. Pull quotes help tell the story for the skimmer and entices them to read more — if you select the right pull quotes. Look for statements or phrases that stand out as being especially powerful, unique or surprising in your copy.

When you build each piece of your campaign on the foundations of direct response copy, you're helping to ensure that you catch the attention of prospects and motivate them to respond.

At best, image-oriented ads help an audience feel good about your product or service, but they do not prompt prospects to make a purchase.

Not only that, traditional advertising copy will kill your campaign.

Likewise, journalistic copy will depress response.

Good direct response copy is easy to recognize because your toll-free phone number is ringing more, your landing page is generating more leads and your sales are soaring.

CHAPTER 20

How to Identify Your Unique Selling Proposition

Your product or service is special. It's unique. You believe that it will change the lives of your prospects for the better … and that it's better than that of the competition.

But can you pinpoint exactly why you believe this?

Can you sum up why your offer is so special in one sentence … or better yet, in just a few words?

If the answer is "No" or even "I'm not sure …" then you haven't identified your Unique Selling Proposition – or USP.

Knowing your USP is critical to effectively marketing your product or service. It's what differentiates your offer from the rest … and makes prospects believe they must buy your product or service.

How do you define your USP?

Plain and simple, your USP is what sets you apart from the competition. How are your products or services better, faster, stronger, easier to use, more profitable or trendier? Your prospect wants to know.

If you don't clearly communicate what you have to offer that no one else does, your prospect won't have a compelling reason to buy from you … instead of choosing a cheaper or more convenient alternative.

If you're not sure what your USP is, finish the statement: "Nowhere else will you find…"

If you have the best pricing on the market, say it. If you're the only company with a certain widget, tell them. If you have the trendiest design, let everyone know it!

In order to define your USP, you might have to take a step back from your product or service.

What I mean is, sometimes you may love your product or service for reasons that aren't necessarily obvious or beneficial to your prospects.

Identify what it is that your product will offer to your prospect that is special and unique ... and how it will change their overall quality of life.

For example, you may sell a meal delivery service. You have lots of competition ... but your meal delivery service may help your prospects lose weight ... and feel happier, more energetic and more attractive as a result.

Your USP is the fact that your service will make prospects happier and healthier than any other competitor on the market.

Now, you've tapped into the psychological benefits of your product – not just the characteristics (like "delivered once weekly," "gluten-free" or "three meals per package").

The USP: The Ultimate Response-Lifter

When your Unique Selling Proposition becomes central to your marketing message, you'll see a dramatic increase in response.

Prospects can understand how your product or service will change their lives ... and why they cannot be happy without it.

That is why you must integrate your USP throughout

all of your marketing materials to lift response in your multichannel, integrated marketing campaign. Remind prospects about your USP again and again .... and tell them that they can get a slimmer body, greater happiness or more energy.

Taking True Religion Jeans from Just a Dream to a Multimillion-Dollar Company

Here's one incredible success story of how I crafted a USP for a denim jean brand that took it from small startup to a multimillion-dollar corporation.

When True Religion Jeans approached me, they were an unknown, start-up company that faced many obstacles to breaking into the cut-throat, denim clothing market.

We overcame two difficult hurdles to make this campaign successful: Because their jeans cost between $150 and $350 a pair, the first hurdle was motivating the consumer to pay the high cost of the jeans and adopt a new favorite brand in a seemingly saturated market.

The second, and perhaps more difficult, hurdle was convincing the retail leaders to clear valuable (and expensive) display space in their stores to promote an unknown company with a small marketing budget.

The solution?

We created a Unique Selling Proposition that set the denim brand apart from competitors and convince prospects to become customers – and high-end stores to carry the brand.

My marketing agency came up with a USP that focused on the unique individuality of True Religion: A healthier, more natural jean where no chemicals were used in its production. This USP promised a pair of jeans that would bring unique comfort and style to the wearer to set them apart.

We stressed benefits such as "sanded by hand to make them smoother, more comfortable and unique … like a piece of art."

Finally, we used phrases like "livable perfection" that elevated the brand from a prized luxury item into an entire lifestyle.

So, we created an entire integrated, multichannel marketing campaign that relied on communicating this powerful USP, including a landing page, a special 3-D marketing campaign to high-end retailers, social media, and data collection pieces.

The results were phenomenal, as True Religion rose to become one of America's most popular denim names and a highly sought-after brand by retailers.

Today, the brand is carried by major luxury retailers, such as Neiman Marcus, Saks Fifth Avenue and Bloomingdale's, and at most high-end retail stores.

And the owner who had only a hope and a dream when he walked through my office door sold his company for $835 million.

Here are four other examples of USP's we developed that helped sales soar.

Chlorella Health Supplement Came to Dominate the Supplement Market

Chlorella is a Japanese health supplement that I helped introduce to the American market by identifying this USP: "Combats the invisible toxic enemy and triggers your body's natural cleansing and revitalizing power."

Over the years we created one of the longest-running, most successful supplement companies in America.

Chlorella touched on prospects' fear of bad health and strong desire for revitalized health.

How *Health Alert* Newsletter Came to Dominate the Health Newsletter Market

Health Alert is a newsletter aimed at the senior market that offers "health solutions that can't be found in a doctor's office."

I launched *Health Alert* when it was just an idea ... and helped turn it into one of the largest alternative health newsletters in America and a multimillion-dollar supplement operation.

Health Alert spoke to older prospects who needed health solutions – not simply prescription meds – to help them live longer, fuller and happier lives.

Vector Vest Online Investment System Came to Dominate Online Investment Services

Vector Vest is an online investment system that "helps

you make the right buy-and-sell decisions 95% of the time."

Another launch that required developing a USP is Vector Vest.

This USP drew on the desire for secure stock market profits ... in other words, the desire for wealth.

We launched and grew this business into the first online investment service in the world.

1-800 Contacts

1-800 Contacts offers contacts that are delivered, meaning prospects "will never have to go to the store again to buy contacts that fit."

1-800 Contacts drew on the desire for ease, convenience and time saved.

All of these USP's stress what's special about the product or service ... and speak to prospects about the life-changing benefits of responding to their offers.

Your USP will be central to your multichannel, integrated marketing campaign.

It's what makes your prospects feel that they must buy from you ... or they have missed a great opportunity to improve their lives.

A good USP can help transform your positioning in the marketplace, set you apart from competitors and, most importantly, help you to see sales skyrocket.

CHAPTER 21

How to Create an Irresistible Offer

Like direct response copy, an irresistible direct response offer is absolutely critical to the success of your multichannel, integrated marketing campaign.

Your landing page, banner ads, emails and other marketing materials should entice your prospects with an opportunity that's almost impossible to resist.

If you're unsure of what an offer is, it's not what you're getting but what the prospect gets.

Remember, your prospects are only human, like you or me. They are only interested in their own needs.

The offer usually includes:

- Pricing: soft/hard offer
- Premiums
- Discounts (sales only)
- A guarantee

In the following chapter, you'll learn how to create an offer that's irresistible to your target audience ... raising overall response and boosting sales for your multichannel, integrated marketing campaign.

Pricing: Price Points, Soft Offers and Hard Offers

Price is a vitally important part of your offer.

A higher price will lower your response. A lower price will increase your response.

But every product or service has its own price point where you get maximum possible profit – and you can only find this optimum price point by testing different price variables.

When setting your pricing, you'll also want to consider whether to make a "soft" offer or a "hard" offer.

A "soft" offer increases your response over a "hard" offer. However, a "soft" offer may not pay off in the long run.

A "soft" offer is where buyers are given the opportunity to order without paying with cash or a credit card before receiving their merchandise. They merely check a box on the order form that reads, "bill me later."

Or if you're generating a lead, a "soft offer" is usually used for an expensive product.

A "hard" offer is an offer where payment by cash or credit card MUST be made with the order before it is shipped.

This strategy is usually used for an inexpensive product requiring payment by credit card.

Premiums: "I Want It More than I Want the Product"

One of the most powerful elements of your offer is the premium.

A premium is a "free" gift or item that's so enticing, your prospects will want to buy your product or service just to get the premium.

Premiums can include:

- Free gift items, such as free food or a household item

- Special reports, checklists or other informational items

- Anything else creative you can think of – early access to a special service, an item signed by the owner or a free ticket to a special event, for example

- Discounts, adding value for prospects by helping them save money

Depending on your business or approach, think creatively about what you can offer potential customers as free incentives to buy from you.

One of my clients, Wine of the Month Club, is a luxury subscription wine delivery service.

As an incentive to subscribe to their monthly service, we crafted an offer for them that included:

- A free bottle of wine, if they joined Wine of the Month Club within 10 days of receiving the direct mail package.

- A reduced price on the first two bottles of wine.

- A free "Wine Explorer's Kit" that included: A cheese board; a seven-part wine education series; a monthly newsletter; a pocket-sized vintage chart to help decode wine menus; and a guide titled "How to speak wine like a pro."

Another client Starshop (a mobile shopping app that taps into celebrity trends), aimed to raise capital from investors. As an incentive to invest in their venture, prospects were offered the opportunity to participate in special events that tie into the company's product line.

This not only caught the interest of investors, it motivated them to respond to an offer that promised so much more than a financial opportunity.

Starshop's offer included:

- Entry to a New Year's Eve Party in Times Square with celebrities, DJs, full bar and a chance to dance the night away.

- Access to a VIP suite at Coachella, a popular music and arts festival in Indio, California.

- Entry to the Grammy's After-Party at the Staples Center in Los Angeles, where investors could mingle with the "Who's Who" of the music industry.

- The chance to go to a movie premiere in Los Angeles and New York with the full red-carpet treatment.

- Three Special Reports for the investor, reinforcing their offer and educating and informing their prospects.

Of course, a few of these value-added pieces may be difficult to use in your own campaign ... But you can still create powerful, response-boosting value-added pieces that don't include access to special events.

One powerful premium that I often put together is a "kit" of special reports.

For a real estate-related offer, I created two special report premiums that the prospect would find worth keeping. The names of these reports were:

- *Secrets to Lower-Risk, Higher-Yield Investing*
- *The Ultimate Guide to Profitably Investing in Real Estate*

I branded these two reports as the "Income Investor Profit Kit."

Ultimately, they helped motivate prospects to make a decision to respond to our client's offer, and helped massively boost response.

If you decide to create special report premiums, it's critical to give these editorial reports powerful titles that offer prospects highly relevant and useful insights or information.

The special report(s) might be two pages long – or 10 pages or 20. They might even be 50 or 100 pages. They could also be formatted as a PowerPoint presentation. Special reports can also be videos or downloads.

Finally, a kit can include a variety of valuable informational pieces, but also a piece that helps explain why your offer is exciting.

Discounts – Increasing the Value of Your Offer

One way to make your prospects feel great about your price and the value of your offer is to include a discount.

People love to hunt for bargains. A discount can be a great motivator that causes your prospects to believe that their purchasing decisions are wise ... not frivolous.

For example, you may want to offer a 10-20% discount on your product or service for a certain period of time ... and make sure to communicate how much money they are saving.

I am selling a book right now, *23 Equity Crowdfunding Secrets to Raising Capital*, and offering a 20% discount – and autographing copies, adding another dimension of value.

The Call-to-Action (CTA): Direct Response Copy for a Powerful Offer

Your CTA should include all critical elements to your offer, including not only the call to purchase from you, but reiterating what prospects will receive when they click on "Buy Now."

This is the same CTA repeated throughout all marketing materials.

On the bottom of the page, you'll see the CTA page from a magalog in a multichannel, integrated marketing campaign.

Note that we gave our prospects three options "Best Deal: Two Years $69," "Great Deal: One Year $39," or "10-Day Quick Response Bonus."

For your multichannel, integrated marketing campaign, you'll want to test different versions of your CTA.

For example, even a simple tweak to your "Purchase" or "Submit" button can make a big difference.

In one test, two checkout pages were tested that were identical in nearly every way, except one had a "Submit button" and

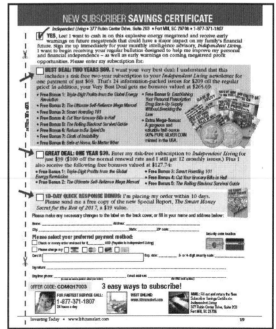

the other had a "Go to Payment Options" button.

When tested, "Go to Payment Options" got a whopping 87.5% more click-thrus than the plain and simple "Submit" button.

Both are commands with an implied you-orientation, but "Go to Payment Options" provides a specific direction that doesn't have the implication or worry of "commitment" behind it.

The CTA is a key step to maximizing your offer and helping ensure that prospects respond "Yes" to purchase from you and receive great value.

Guarantees: Increasing Trust (and Response)

The higher your price, the stronger your guarantee should be. A strong guarantee helps increase your marketing response.

A typical guarantee that I make for subscription services is called a "Triple Money-Back Guarantee."

In this guarantee, customers get their money back if they're not satisfied ... and they get to keep the first product or service they received, along with the premium.

This kind of assurance communicates that you are absolutely sure that your prospects will be satisfied.

And, it helps increase overall response by lowering the risk factor of buying.

What you offer to the prospect – and how well you communicate it – is absolutely critical to your success.

Think strategically and creatively about your pricing, premiums, CTA, discount and guarantee – and you'll see your response skyrocket!

CHAPTER 22

The Power of Value-Added Marketing

What is value-added marketing?

Value-added marketing is the powerful boost you give to your multichannel, integrated marketing campaign that completely changes the tone, approach and feel of your offer.

It does this by communicating to your prospects that you are there to give, not take from them.

Simply put, value-added marketing offers your prospects something that they think is in their self-interest:

Something valuable.

Something objective.

Something that creates high interest.

Value-added marketing includes a gift or free information that educates and informs the prospect ... and that also offers powerful motivation to purchase your item and become a loyal customer.

In fact, I created a powerful system called V.I.V.A. that acts as a powerful foundation of any value-added marketing.

V.I.V.A. relies on two principles:

Valuable information: First, value-added marketing must include information that the prospect will find valuable. This is content that is actionable, insightful or surprising – or all three.

Value-added: Second, value-added marketing entices your prospects by making them feel they are getting something for free. It increases the overall value of your offer by making it more difficult to resist.

Value-added marketing can help elevate your offer and ensure the success of your campaign in the following four ways:

1. Convince skeptical prospects that you're trustworthy.

Your prospects automatically think that you're selling them something.

When that happens, they're likely to not even want to discover what you have to offer. For example, they won't look at your mailing piece to learn about your product or service because they don't think there's anything in it for them.

Value-added marketing helps to override that initial skepticism and persuade prospects to consider your offer.

2. A value-added component will help get your advertising or marketing effort read ... and generate a response.

When you offer something of value to prospects, they are more likely to rip open your envelope, click on your ad or open your email.

Take direct mail. Most direct mail does not have a value-added component. But when you add it, you'll increase your response.

Take a look at the envelope on the next page, created for a Wine of the Month Club campaign.

Note that the envelope says, "Do Not Bend: Free Checklist Enclosed" – a suggestive way to communicate that something valuable is inside that will be theirs just by opening the envelope.

The "Free Checklist" was a special piece with "7 Things You Should Never, Ever Do at a Wine Tasting" – a fun extra that wine aficionados would appreciate.

3. **Value-added advertising helps create the relationships with prospects and clients you must have for successful marketing.**

By offering high-value advertising for free, you create a sense of trust with prospects … helping to build valuable relationships that turn prospects into customers and current customers into loyal, longtime buyers.

4. **Value-added marketing can be used on most marketing channels to achieve great success.**

I've used value-added marketing in email, landing pages, native ads, direct mail and more.

It's giving – not taking. And it results in greater sales.

Valued-Added Marketing: What Will You Offer?

Value-added marketing is a critical tool for building strong relationships with your prospects and customers ... and boosting your response.

Next, consider what kind of value-added advertising tactic you will want to use.

One example of a direct mail package that uses value-added marketing to build and strengthen relationship was for a Christian organization called "The Navigators." They put together a direct mail piece for Christmas that included the following free gifts:

- Personalized return address stickers
- A booklet of Christmas carols
- Christmas-themed envelope seals
- A Christmas-themed desk calendar
- A personalized certificate of appreciation
- A "Christmas Fun" booklet

Of course, this was a very extensive value-added campaign, with multiple pieces. But they understood that adding value to an offer builds valuable relationships – ultimately lifting response, and most importantly, increasing profits.

CHAPTER 23

The New Credibility

A critical part of your multichannel, integrated marketing campaign is to help overcome your prospects' objections and skepticism.

Seven out of 10 prospects who visit your landing page or receive your direct mail piece will be skeptical about whether you are telling them the truth about your offer.

That's why it's up to you to immediately overcome that skepticism by establishing your credibility.

The New Credibility: Persuading Your Prospects That You Mean What You Say

The new credibility means that you use multiple ways to convince your prospects that your offer will be worth their time and money.

The new credibility is the key to help "close the deal" on your sale.

Here are six ways you can help establish credibility on your landing page, direct mail piece, emails and other marketing elements of your multichannel, integrated campaign.

1. Use star ratings to show customer satisfaction.

Use a 4- or 5-star rating to help prospects see how satisfied other customers have been with your product or service.

You can display the star rating on your landing

page or direct mail piece, with an image of your product or service.

Star ratings make an immediate impact on your prospects by showing simple, straightforward evidence of the quality as rated by others of your product or service.

Here is a powerful example from a newsalog we created for *Health Alert* – an alternative health newsletter.

Joseph Sharone
PSORIASIS
RATED: ★ ★ ★ ★ ★

Joseph Sharone

"Dear Dr. West, your *Health Alert* newsletter gives me all the latest health news. Before starting your protocol, I would scratch my psoriasis spots in my sleep until they bled, what a mess. My psoriasis improved so much that I'm not scratching any more. What a blessing Dr. West's protocol has been for me. Thanks again. Dr. West!"

—*Joseph Sharone, Florida*

2. Video testimonials show your credibility in action.

When prospects see live video footage of satisfied customers talking about your product or service, they are far more likely to trust your credibility.

Plus, video will boost your overall results – your prospects will enjoy watching different testimonials on your landing page or in your digital ads.

3. Reviews will be carefully read – and believed – by potential customers.

A more traditional approach to testimonials is to show multiple reviews from customers (with star ratings included).

Include reviews of happy, satisfied customers on your landing page – many of your prospects will take the time to read them. In fact, 85% of prospects read up to 10 reviews before purchasing a product or service.

4. Build your credibility with your pre-heads and captions.

Use powerful pre-heads and captions that cite credible outside sources to affirm the trustworthiness of your offer.

Here are some pre-heads and captions that help build credibility and create intrigue:

- **Former IRS agent and best selling author reveals...**

- **After 25 years of research, Lawrence Livermore National Laboratory engineer creates software breakthrough...**

- **As seen in... (Tech Weekly, Software Review Magazine, etc...)**

5. Positive reviews on Amazon are powerful response-boosters.

If you sell your product or service on Amazon,

Paul Peters
SINUSITIS / CHRONIC RHINOSINUSITIS
RATED: ★ ★ ★ ★ ★

"I've had serious sinus problems for as long as I can remember, and they sometimes lay me up for weeks at a time. I tried over-the-counter medicine and antibiotics but they didn't work at all. It was only when I found Dr. Bruce West and his *Health Alert* newsletter that I was able to get any relief.

Paul Peters

His natural protocols put an end to an ongoing sinus infection, and then I stopped getting them altogether.

"Your doctor will never tell you about these natural protocols because he doesn't know about them. So now I tell everyone I know to read *Health Alert* and Dr. West's Doctor's A-Z Phytoceutical Guide to find evidence-based natural solutions for their problems."

—*Paul Peters, Connecticut*

make sure that your satisfied customers are leaving you reviews.

Amazon reviews are considered powerful credibility pieces. They will be even more likely to be read than your product description.

Encourage your current customers to leave reviews with retargeting emails and digital ads.

6. Give prospects the option for a "live chat."

Showing that you have excellent customer service is key to your credibility.

Now, you can offer prospects the option of actually talking with a customer service representative (or "chatbot") using a live chat option on your landing page.

Prospects are more likely to trust your offer when they have the option of talking to a representative "live."

Your credibility is critical to getting a high response with your multichannel, integrated marketing campaign.

Prospects need to believe what you say – and trust that your product or service is high-quality.

Part Five

Multichannel, Integrated Strategies and Tactics to Boost Response

In the final four chapters (24–28), you'll learn critical foundations to your multichannel, integrated campaign.

These include key tactics – such as using a targeted landing page and creating a direct response video – that will help you take your multichannel, integrated campaign to the next level.

CHAPTER 24

Your Landing Page: The Foundation of Your Multichannel, Integrated Marketing Campaign – 12 Critical Rules

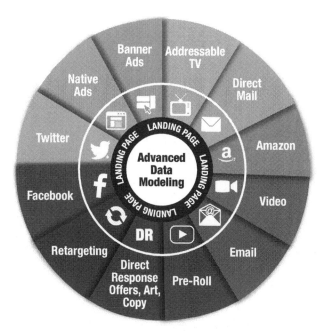

Your landing page is foundational to your multichannel, integrated marketing campaign.

Why?

Because it is the "landing place" seen by your prospects or customers.

And the landing place should not be your "corporate

website" or a website filled with graphics but devoid of copy.

When prospects click on Facebook ads, they will be taken to your landing page.

When they click on a link in an email, they will be taken to your landing page.

When they click on "Find Out More" after a pre-roll video, they will be taken to your landing page.

The message they see matches the sales message on the Facebook advertising, emails and pre-roll videos.

This specifically targeted sales message will maximize your response, producing the leads and sales you want.

That's why it's so critical to create an effective landing page.

Otherwise, you will experience mediocre results and a depressed response.

Don't make this fatal mistake!

A fatal mistake for any marketer is to rely on your corporate website – instead of a landing page – to drive your sales.

Corporate websites tend to depress response by confusing prospects with too many choices and decisions to make. Multiple messages and navigation bars drive prospects away from the page … without getting them to click on "buy now."

Without a singular focus on your products or service message, you'll experience a greatly reduced response.

In fact, most corporate websites are anti-marketing sites that do too much … and don't help you sell.

That's why the landing page is so important. A good landing page does not have navigation distractions. It presents a single message that is clear and simple. It has a focused unique selling proposition (USP) and call-to-action (CTA) and drives the prospect to respond.

And, the landing page has copy and art that complement the marketing materials and nothing else.

Remember, prospects don't want to have to think too hard when they come to your page. They make quick judgments to read on or move on, based on how well the page matches the ad they responded to. Make sure your product and offer are clear and upfront.

Otherwise, they'll leave your page – probably forever.

To an ad agency or graphic web designer, a landing page like this can look pretty boring. But for the prospect, it's what helps generate high response … and ultimately, profits.

12 Critical Rules for an Effective Landing Page

Here are 12 foundational rules to keep in mind when creating an effective landing page for your multichannel, integrated campaign:

#1: Use a powerful, highly targeted headline.

Your headline is critical to drawing the prospect in and making sure they don't leave. It should be written to show how your offer will benefit your specific audience, and create curiosity, benefit and drama or suspense.

#2: Use mobile and desktop versions.

It is very important to optimize your landing page for mobile phones, as you learned about in Chapter 13.

That's because most of your prospects will use their mobile phones, rather than a desktop or laptop computer, to look at your landing page.

In fact, 62% of all mobile users make purchases on their cell phones – and 80% of shoppers use their phones to look up products or services before making a purchase.

Having few navigational distractions and a clear call-to-action will help ensure that your landing page is optimized for a mobile phone. Consider presenting your copy as a "list" of easily readable points: This will help streamline your message and make it easier to read.

And always, always, always test your landing page on both a desktop and a mobile device before running it. Driving prospects away from your page will cost you in sales and profits.

#3: Break copy into numerical points.

Break copy up into a list of numerical points. For example, "6 Things You Must Know About CBD Oil Now." This makes it easier to scan and understand, especially for readers who are "skimmers" (those who skim the copy, without fully reading it).

#4: Don't break copy up with images.

Use graphics to help direct eye flow to the copy – not to distract readers from reading your offer.

#5: Use direct response copy.

As you learned about in Chapter 19, direct response copy is a scientific, measurable approach to advertising that relies on "you-oriented" copy that stresses the unique benefits – not the features – of your product or service.

It's key that you use only direct response copy on

your landing page – otherwise, you will drive prospects away from the page. The copy on your landing page will also reinforce the exciting offer that is in your mailing package, banner ads, emails and other marketing materials.

As I explained earlier, direct response copy is often longer than what you might normally see on a website, email or ad.

But it gets a higher response – and persuades the prospect to respond to act on your unique offer.

#6: Show a clear call-to-action (CTA).

Remember, your landing page has one clear purpose: to drive the prospect to respond to your offer. That's your call-to-action (CTA), and it should be presented clearly.

The CTA should be made clear on top of the landing page, and should be repeated multiple times throughout the page.

#7: Use retargeting to powerfully boost response.

As you learned about in Chapter 7, retargeting uses cookies on your landing page to "follow" your prospects around the web with digital ads, including banner ads and Facebook ads. This is a critical part of your marketing program that will increase response and drive prospects back to the landing page.

#8: Include a video.

Video adds a powerful element to your landing page by creating drama and delivering a high-impact message to the prospect. Video has been shown to significantly increase viewer response by as much as 80% for a landing page.

Here are a few quick tips for effectively using video

on your landing page:

1. Place your video at the top of the page – it should be the first thing prospects see when they visit your landing page. Even if they don't watch it, it still gives your product or service greater credibility.

2. Place an attention-grabbing, benefit-oriented headline just above the video – and a powerful caption under it.

3. In the first 12 seconds of the video, promise something big and unusual to your prospects.

You can also offer a transcript of the video directly on your landing page for prospects who prefer to read the video script.

You'll learn more about creating powerful video in Chapter 27.

#9: Use direct response art.

Just like your copy, your graphics should invite your prospects to respond. Graphics should reinforce your big idea and not create unnecessary distractions.

Direct response art is the science of creating "eye-flow" to encourage and maximize readership ... and ultimately, response.

#10: Show credibility.

It's critical that your landing page shows the credibility of your product or service.

One of the most powerful ways to convince prospects of your credibility is to show customer testimonials.

Use customer reviews. Amazon revolutionized the buying process by showing customer reviews on every single product page.

In fact, they have made testimonials and reviews so

customary that, if you don't include them, prospects may be turned off and leave your page.

You can show satisfied customer testimonials in a number of ways: for example, as a video, or a picture of the testimonial given with their quote below it.

Star ratings are also an effective way to increase the effectiveness of your testimonials or reviews.

"Wow" prospects with killer testimonials and reviews on your landing page, and you'll help persuade them that they absolutely cannot live without your product or service.

#11: Optimize for search engines (SEO).

Many people think that if your website is not a .gov, .edu or a news website, your site won't be easily searchable.

In reality, these types of sites don't rank well in search engines, because they are poorly optimized. But with the right Search Engine Optimization (SEO), your page can show up more easily in organic search results.

Here are six critical foundations for your landing page SEO:

1. SEO keywords

These are the words and phrases that help people find your page through an organic search. Your focus keywords should be highly relevant to your content and optimized for your ideal audience.

Strategically place SEO keywords in your copy – such as in the first paragraph of your copy, in your site title and in subheads. But don't "keyword stuff." Using keywords needlessly, in places that don't make sense, won't work to improve SEO. Search algorithms are smarter than that.

2. Title tags

These are the titles that appear on search engine results pages. Your title tags should be between 55 and 60 characters, and clear and descriptive of what's on your page. Include your SEO keywords in your title tag.

3. Meta descriptions

Meta descriptions are the brief descriptions shown on search engine results pages. Your meta description should be under 160 characters and include SEO keywords.

4. Alt text

Use alt text for any graphics you may include on your page. Alt text may not be displayed to the user, but it will improve your SEO.

5. 301 redirects

If you are creating a new page that will replace an older one, use "301 redirects" so that when you remove the old page, the SEO value remains. 301 redirects let your prospects know that the page has been moved, and provide the link to the newer page.

These five SEO foundations will help you get a good start on optimizing your landing page for search engines.

6. External links

Build links into your external landing page to relevant sites.

When other sites link to your landing page that's even better.

Both are great for improving your SEO.

#12: Use a floater

A floater is a marketing tool that sends a form that "floats up" over a website or landing page. Most think they are the old "pop-ups" … and they are similar, but they don't open a new window.

Floaters can appear in different formats, shapes and sizes – including a "slide-in" floater or transparent floater.

Typically, the form is used for data collection. It can also show a special offer or discount (which later links to data collection). Usually, I'll use it to collect a name and email address by offering a free special report.

The floater form asks a user to enter in their contact information: name, email, and sometimes phone number or address.

Here's an example of a floater I created for my own marketing newsletter update:

Floaters are powerful, because they help you collect a highly responsive database to convert visitors into leads and sales.

Leads then receive your emails, see your digital ads and receive your direct mail, and they are much more likely to become customers … loyal customers that purchase from you again and again.

STAY ONE STEP AHEAD!

Direct Marketing Update is your key to the latest direct response advertising and marketing breakthroughs, strategies and trends authored by legendary marketing guru Craig Huey.

Don't miss one weekly issue filled with concise tactics, case studies, test results and tips all delivered to your inbox.

Craig Huey, President of CDMG.

First Name *
Enter first name

Last Name *
Enter last name

Email *
Enter your email

Company
Enter company

Phone Number *
Enter phone number

SUBSCRIBE

Floaters enable you to collect valuable data, to expand your prospect base and to build powerful custom lists that will help you multiply your profits and grow your business.

This is not an optional marketing tool – floaters are key to your success.

As with any marketing piece, it's critical that you test different types of floaters with different copy to determine what will get the best response.

Now, let's take a look at landing pages I've completed using the principles I've outlined on previous pages …

Powerful landing pages I've created for clients

Here are examples of effective landing pages I've provided to clients:

Allegiancy

I created the following landing page for "Allegiancy," a client looking to find investors for an equity crowdfunding campaign.

Strategically, no navigation options exist.

This headline creates intrigue and helps motivate visitors to continue reading.

There is also a call-to-action in the upper-right-hand corner of the page. It's also listed further down the page, giving prospects multiple opportunities to respond to the call-to-action.

Note the strong headline at the top: *Breaking: New Disruptive Technology on the Verge of "Blowing Up" a $15 Trillion Industry.*

But again, there is only one call-to-action.

The copy may look longer than is typical for a website – but this will actually increase viewer response.

Breaking: New, Disruptive Technology On the Verge of "Blowing Up" a $15 Trillion Industry

Why Smart Investors Are Getting in on This "Mini-IPO" <u>Before</u> Wall Street

The Last Company to Offer this "Mini-IPO" Saw its Shares Soar 525% in Just a Matter of Days – Will this Company Be the Next?

Year	Projected Assets Under Management
2016	$1 billion
2017	$2.8 billion
2018	$4.8 billion
2019	$6.8 billion
2020	$8.8 billion
2021	$10.8 billion

On the next page, see another landing page I created for my client, "SuperFood Weight Loss."

The video is prominent and easy to see.

Also, notice the "spokesperson" – in this case, the owner of the company – in the upper left corner.

A spokesperson helps create both trust and credibility for the prospect, increasing the chances that he or she will respond to your offer.

The spokesperson may be the owner of the company,

a celebrity or someone else who is relevant to the product or service (such as an investment analyst for an investment newsletter).

You'll learn more about how to choose a spokesperson in Chapter 25.

Here's a quick recap of what your landing page should

include to be effective:

- 🌐 No navigational distractions
- 🌐 One clear CTA
- 🌐 Direct response copy and art
- 🌐 Video
- 🌐 Retargeting
- 🌐 Testimonials
- 🌐 Optimize for mobile devices

Do not neglect your landing page. If you want to maximize your profits and increase your conversion rate, then you absolutely must get your landing page right. Your landing page is your closer. It's up to your landing page to break through your prospect's skepticism and make you money.

Your landing page is your last line of defense before the prospect clicks away and is lost forever. If it's sub-par, then you will have wasted your time, money, and effort on all marketing materials that drive prospects to the landing page.

Remember to use the elements above to ensure that you have an effective landing page – and a strong foundation for your multichannel, integrated marketing campaign.

CHAPTER 25

New Breakthroughs in Shopping Cart Abandonment

You might think that by the time a prospect has placed an item in your digital shopping cart, it's a done deal – you've made a sale.

Unfortunately, that's not the case.

More than seven out of 10 people abandon their shopping carts without completing a purchase. In 2017, online merchants lost around $7 trillion from shopping cart abandonment alone.

Why?

Potential customers get sidelined by navigation distractions. Or, the purchase process is too complicated. Shoppers get distracted and confused – and you lose a sale.

5 Keys to Creating a High-Response Shopping Cart

Optimizing your shopping cart is critical to increasing profits from your multichannel, integrated marketing campaign.

After all, your campaign may have been successful in driving prospects to your landing page, and finally to a purchase.

But if the shopping cart is unsuccessful, all your efforts will be wasted.

Here are five keys to creating a high-response shopping

cart that will reduce shopping cart abandonment and boost sales from your multichannel, integrated marketing campaign:

1. Keep it simple with one or two steps.

The more steps that are required to purchase items in your shopping cart, the more likely it is that a potential customer will abandon the transaction.

Keep your purchase process simple, with only one or two steps.

Customers should be able to make a purchase by filling out the minimum amount of information.

2. Get rid of navigation distractions.

If your shopping cart page offers multiple opportunities to do something other than make a purchase, then your prospects are likely to get distracted.

Keep your shopping cart simple and streamlined, with one action to perform: Buy your product or service.

3. Offer your prospects a premium and guarantee.

A premium (as discussed in Chapter 21) makes buying your product or service more enticing – and decreases the chances that prospects will abandon their purchase.

Remind prospects of the special item, report or bonus they will receive if they buy from you.

And, remember to include a guarantee: A money-back offer within a certain time frame if they aren't satisfied with their product or service.

A "Double Risk Free Guarantee" is shown on the next page.

4. Include a Positive Acceptance Statement (PAS).

A positive acceptance statement (PAS) helps customers make a decision to buy from you.

It helps prevent your multichannel, integrated marketing campaign from falling short of its anticipated response.

You may recognize a PAS as the "Yes" box. But more importantly, it is the section of the order form where your prospect can read a recap of what he or she gets in return for responding. It is a powerful statement that should motivate even the most reluctant prospect to say, "Yes, I want your product in order to sleep better at night. Sign me up!"

Using a PAS on your shopping cart will affirm your prospect's decision and dramatically reduce the chance of abandonment.

NEW SUBSCRIBER **SAVINGS CERTIFICATE**

Independent Living • 377 Rubin Center Drive, Suite 203 • Fort Mill, SC 29708 • 1-877-371-1807

YES, Lee! I want to cash in on this explosive energy megatrend and receive early warnings on future megatrends that could have a major impact on my family's financial future. Sign me up immediately for your monthly intelligence advisory, *Independent Living*. I want to begin receiving your regular bulletins designed to help me improve my personal and financial independence – as well as early warnings on coming megatrend profit opportunities. Please enter my subscription for:

5. Retarget prospects who abandon their shopping cart.

You can still recapture customers who abandon their shopping cart with retargeting emails and ads.

Retargeting is a powerful strategy that reminds potential prospects of what they forgot about in their shopping cart.

First, prospects who have abandoned their shopping cart receive a follow-up email.

The subject line might be, "Did you forget something?" – or something similar.

Then, these prospects will be retargeted with Facebook, banner ads and native ads that "follow" them around the internet. Similarly to the emails, these ads could display an image of what they left in their shopping cart, reminding them of what they forgot.

Retargeting is a powerful strategy to help shopping cart "abandoners" complete their purchase.

CHAPTER 26

The Key Question: Your Spokesperson

Your spokesperson is one of your critical keys to success that will help you generate leads and get prospects to respond to your offer.

Your spokesperson is your "voice" for generating the lead – and your voice in the conversion process.

You may not have even thought about having a spokesperson yet ... or thought of choosing a spokesperson for your campaign.

But consider the following questions:

- Who will sign the direct mail letter or email?
- Whose picture will you place on the landing page? Will you use one?
- Who will be the voice of the company?
- Who will be your spokesperson or personality?
- Who will be the people or star in your TV commercial or video?

These choices will significantly affect response to your campaign, and can make the difference between a campaign that generates massive revenue and one that fails to get a response.

Some marketers do not want to use a spokesperson. When I have a client taking this position, I honor their decision. But I stress that their campaign should at least be tested with a spokesperson.

I almost always see a spokesperson being effective. Though I admit, on rare occasions, it doesn't work well. In fact, it's embarrassing to have to tell a company president that his or her image depresses response.

But usually, it helps.

Charles Schwab once said that the best thing he did was use his image in all the marketing for his company – it gave him a competitive advantage.

Who Should You Choose as Your Spokesperson

Depending on your product or service, you should choose your spokesperson strategically.

For some clients, I recommend that they choose the company's president, such as clients using a marketing campaign to raise capital for their venture.

For companies selling an alternative health product, you may want to use a doctor, even if they are not part of the company. It brings credibility to your message.

For companies selling a financial service, you may want to use an outside, independent certified public accountant (CPA) or financial writer.

For companies selling a food or beverage product, you may want to use a chef, sommelier or other type of specialist.

Be creative. There are some types of spokespersons I do not recommend, however.

I do not typically recommend celebrities, unless they are highly relevant to your product or service. They are seldom worth the price. I also do not recommend your vice president of marketing or sales. Those titles alone will depress response.

Consider what kind of spokesperson will provide the most credibility and build relationships with your prospects. Remember, your spokesperson must look and seem like a "real" person, not like an overly polished actor who isn't relatable.

Personality: The Little-Known Way to Increase Response

It may seem controversial or even counterintuitive, but you may want to feature your spokesperson on all of your marketing materials – such as the landing page, magalog, direct mail envelope and digital ads.

It's been proven time and time again that one of the little-known ways to increase response with consumers or business-to-business campaigns is to have a personality who represents your marketing campaign.

By using a photo of your spokesperson, you will be more likely to build trust in your service or product with your prospects and customers.

Look at this letter I created for the Wine of the Month Club, to the right:

On the next page, see an example of a Thank you page I created for an investment newsletter service, with the investment newsletter writer. These types of

marketing materials get great response for my clients ... and proved that the seemingly risky choice of using a spokesperson was the right one.

Thank you!

I've got your back...

Hi, I'm Lee Bellinger, founder of Independent Living News. I'm so glad you decided to join us. It is my belief that informed individuals who truly love freedom are the foundation of this country. I will do everything in my power to help you live a more safe, secure and self-reliant life.

Yours in freedom,

Lee Bellinger

Back to the home page

Your spokesperson is critical to your multichannel, integrated marketing campaign. Consider this choice carefully as you develop your content and your approach.

CHAPTER 27

Video: A Critical, Powerful Key to Your Multichannel, Integrated Marketing Campaign – 21 Critical Rules

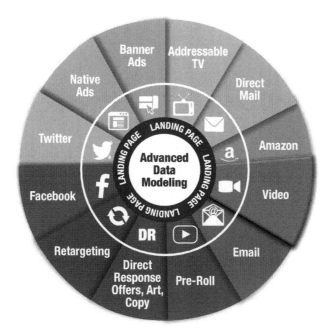

Video communicates your offer unlike any other market medium.

Video brings your product or service to life with demonstrations, testimonials and benefits in action. It's a powerful way to deliver your message to prospects – and generate leads and sales.

Video also lends credibility to your offer, a critical key to earning the trust of potential customers.

I love video. In fact, I started my career in TV commercials, and I've created over 400 videos and TV commercials (including 13 infomercials). I have seen the effectiveness and power of this media, again and again.

For a multichannel, integrated marketing campaign, I create video to be used on the landing page, digital ads, pre-roll video ads, email and in some cases, direct response TV.

In this chapter, you'll discover how to create persuasive, high-impact video.

You'll also learn about using this video in different ways, including in pre-roll ads and for direct response TV.

After creating hundreds of videos for clients, I've developed specific strategies and insights for creating effective, response-boosting video content.

Here are 21 critical rules for video that will help you produce outstanding results and get the response you're looking for.

Rule #1: The first few seconds of your video are key.

You've got to capture the attention of your prospect immediately. It's easy to skip a video, so make sure the first few seconds are powerful, and deliver your message clearly.

Don't start with a fade-in from a black screen – instead, use vibrant, colorful images to immediately engage the viewer.

Rule #2: Use only direct response copy and art in your script.

Your script should have one clear theme. It must be benefit-oriented and guide your viewer through the principles of AIDA: It should draw attention, attract interest, develop desire and compel action.

Remember, the video needs to use direct response copy to produce a high response. This is not the time to use journalistic or traditional advertising copy. That would kill the sale. Your video is a story designed to get people to buy your product or service, or generate that lead.

Likewise, use only direct response art. In a video, direct response art includes:

- No reverse type: White text on a black background decreases readability and response.

- Readability: Make sure that any text is easy for your prospect to read and understand quickly. Bullet points are an effective way to communicate information quickly.

- Avoid navigation distractions: Don't distract your viewers with options to navigate away from the video. Your video has one goal: To drive prospects to respond to a call-to-action (CTA).

Rule #3: Use a credible spokesperson to demonstrate benefits.

Seeing the benefits in action – and hearing the opportunity discussed by the spokesperson – are powerful.

A spokesperson can be more effective than sheer entertainment … but that doesn't mean your video can't be fun. For example, I cast a 4-year old as "the world's greatest investment trader" in a client's online video. It was entertaining, informative and effective.

Rule #4: Repeat your unique selling proposition (USP).

Just as you should feature your USP at the beginning, in the middle and at the end of every print campaign, you also need it in your video. Be sure it's consistent with the rest of your branding and collateral materials.

Rule #5: Don't distract your viewers.

Don't distract your prospects with effects or details that might be "entertaining," but don't cause them to respond to your offer.

Keep your video simple. It should clearly communicate your Unique Selling Proposition (USP) and compel your viewer to action.

Rule #6: PowerPoint v. action.

The video style that is the most effective for a target audience is a video with PowerPoint words, or something called a "storybook" video. Using text with video increases retention and response. For Facebook, this strategy also gives you an advantage in increasing your reach.

Rule #7: Use text.

Whether you're using a live personality or a PowerPoint, you can use on-screen text to lengthen the time that a prospect will watch a video – and how likely they are to respond to your offer. Make sure that the words properly reflect what's being said, are easy to read and stay in one location.

Facebook actually says that using printed words increases video engagement by an average of 12%. If you're not sure how to add text to your video, Facebook has a tool that makes it easy to add word captions to your videos.

Rule #8: Use testimonials and/or reviews with ratings.

Testimonials are one of the most powerful sales tools in existence. But remember, prospects want to see real people who like your product.

Showing a person who is not a professional actor or model – someone who seems uncomfortable and whose story is not overly rehearsed – actually increases your response.

When you're filming customer testimonials, shoot them several times so you can edit exactly what you want from the answers. iPhone testimonials are great, too!

Rule #9: Connect the script with the prospect quickly and dramatically.

Like the copy you use for direct mail, email and other marketing materials, a powerful direct response script will hit hard immediately.

Drama. Suspense. Surprise. No warm-up. No introduction. Command attention.

Remember … 47% of the value of a video is delivered within the first three seconds, and 74% in the first 10.

Rule #10: Length – fear not.

Do not be afraid of a longer video. Some of the most powerful videos are 12 minutes long. When considering video length, ask yourself the following questions: How complicated are your benefits to explain? How easy is it to overcome objections?

For a multichannel, integrated campaign, I normally create three-to-12 minute videos.

Rule #11: Get a model release.

Always get a model release from those you're filming

so you have the right to use your footage wherever you want to, whether that be on your landing page, Facebook, banner ads or elsewhere. You may also want to use footage in creative ways, for example using a still photo and an excerpt from the testimonial in a brochure.

Rule #12: Have a strong call-to-action (CTA).

Your job is to make it as easy as possible for the viewer to respond ... whether you show a phone number, email address, URL or mailing address.

Rule #13: Graphics add power.

The addition of graphics in the right places will increase viewer retention and reinforce your message. Every image must reflect the value of your offer.

Rule #14: Optimize your video for silent mode.

Believe it or not, 85% of people watch Facebook videos on silent. That means that you'll have to create drama and impact without relying on a voiceover or background music.

Instead, communicate your message with powerful action and show important words as text on screen.

Rule #15: Clean and simple win on small screens.

Remember that many of your prospects will be watching your video on mobile screens. Avoid small text and detailed visuals, and keep your graphics simple and bold. This is a key detail when choosing your thumbnail image, which should be clean and bright to catch the eye of your viewers.

Your title doesn't need to be included in the thumbnail – you can attach metadata to the file when you share it online.

Rule #16: The camera is unforgiving.

Consider how the subjects you're filming appear

through the lens. Don't neglect wardrobe considerations. An outrageously patterned tie or an electric blue dress can distract viewers from the content.

Take extra time to see what doesn't belong in the shot. For example, a newspaper or magazine showing a headline can immediately date your production and limit its use.

Rule #17: Remember Murphy's Law. If something can go wrong, it will.

Plan, plan, plan! If you don't bring it to your video shoot, you're sure to need it. If you don't have a Plan B, you'll need one. Outline everything you'll need, including rolls and rolls of duct tape, and take special care with cameras and other equipment that may become victims of carelessness.

Look into getting insurance for the day of the shoot that includes weather, equipment and both personal and corporate liability.

Rule #18: Allow for extra shots.

Always shoot more footage than you need, since you'll always need more than you thought. Even if you think a scene is "perfect," shoot a backup so you can pick from the best material as you edit.

Make time for "establishing shots" – shots that show the context of what's being sold. Shoot "reaction shots" to show one person reacting to another's comments. This is called "B-roll" footage, which can be invaluable during editing.

Rule #19: Maximize its use.

Brainstorm multiple uses for your video – as a premium, as a download or to drive prospects to your URL. Use a screenshot of your video for emails, banner ads and native ads. You'll want to choose a screenshot that teases with powerful words that increase click-through.

Rule #20: Enlist the right crew.

Remember, it was direct response marketers who perfected the infomercial. And the infomercial is still highly effective today.

It's important to use direct response marketing professionals, not video professionals or general ad agencies, to get the most out of your video.

Rule #21: Have a transcript "read-through."

Provide a transcript of your video so that prospects have the option of reading through the video content as well as watching it. A written transcript increases the impact of the video – and multiplies response.

With these rules, you'll be ready to create your video component of your multichannel, integrated campaign.

Videos will be an essential as they are a powerful way to communicate your offer, increase response, gain credibility and win new leads and prospects.

CHAPTER 28

Testing to Maximize Results

Imagine that you've developed and deployed your multichannel, integrated marketing campaign – including a landing page, direct mail package, email, Facebook and banner ads, video and retargeting strategy.

But you're not finished yet…

Now comes one of the most decisive parts of your campaign: Testing.

Testing can make the difference between marketing efforts that disappoint and marketing efforts that produce outstanding, profit-boosting results.

Testing is the cornerstone of any direct response marketing campaign. Every component of direct marketing media must be accountable and measurable.

That's why I call direct response marketing "Accountable Advertising" or "Scientific Advertising."

Always test.

Testing reduces your risk, gives you valuable marketing intelligence for the future and allows you to constantly increase your response rate.

By testing, you'll learn the following key details:

- You will always know when you spend a dollar and when you receive or earn a dollar … or 75¢ or $1.50.
- You always know your cost-per-lead.
- You always know your cost-per-sale.

With any kind of media – direct mail, Facebook, banner ads, email – you'll always know the cost and return on the investment.

Testing for Your Multichannel, Integrated Marketing Campaign

It's absolutely essential to test every element of your multichannel, integrated marketing campaign, using A/B tests to determine the kind of copy, imagery, and other variables that get the most favorable response.

You can test headlines, components, email subject lines, different landing pages, landing page headlines, banner ads, different email lists, even price points ... hundreds of variables.

When I put together a campaign, I always choose carefully what to test.

In the following pages, I'll show you four different tests that reveal how changing a variable can affect response.

Direct Mail Campaign: Postal List and Envelope Test

Here is a powerful example of an envelope test I performed for a direct mail campaign.

This test consisted of about 60,000 pieces.

In this example, I tested two essential response boosters of the campaign:

1. The postal lists I used

2. The envelope copy, or teaser copy, for which I created two versions: Version A and Version B

I sent two versions of teaser copy to nine different lists.

- 60,000-piece mailing, nine different lists
- 30,000 version "A" vs. 30,000 version "B"
- Universe of potential names: 2,965,422

Here are the results of the test:

	Teaser Version A response rate %	Teaser Version B response rate %
List 1	.61	.69
List 2	.40	.34
List 3	.60	.73
List 4	.55	.60
List 5	.36	.46
List 6	.42	.55
List 7	.71	.79
List 8	.65	.72
List 9	.69	.78
Average	List: A 55.4%	List B: 62.8%

As you can see, Version B produced more returns ... and became the "control."

With this test, I identified which were the best-performing mailing lists and which version of the teaser copy worked best.

Let's say that first, you required a .55 to justify your campaign, and then you only use those list cells performing above a .60.

Second, you can see that Version B significantly outperformed Version A. So, you'll mail Version B and forget about Version A.

Based on what you learn, you'll create a new Version

"C" to beat Version "B."

American Express Publishing: Adjusting the Price to Increase Response

One of the reasons it's so important to test different variables is that the results of a test may surprise you.

Here's a test that American Express Publishing performed for one of their publications:

Starting with a control price of $19.95, American Express compared these three price points to its control price.

- $19.97
- $19.99
- $19.49

The average customer might guess that the cheapest price got the highest response rate – $19.49.

But in reality, the highest price got the most response.

Results: If you guessed $19.99 you are right! Offered at that price, compared to the control price of $19.95, the price of $19.99 resulted in 10% better sales. The worst price point was actually the lowest price: $19.49.

Magalog Cover Test: SurfControl Security Software

SurfControl is a provider of corporate security software that came to me with a challenge: Help them sell their product, SuperScout, in a competitive market with such heavy hitters as Norton.

To set SuperScout apart, we created a magalog that persuaded the CEO/CFO/top-level corporate prospects of the value and specific benefits of using SuperScout.

But to ensure the best possible results for SurfControl, we produced two different covers to test in the market.

Here is cover A:

And, cover B *(Next Page)*:

In this case, both the headline and graphics were different on each cover.

Cover A says, "How Fortune 1000 Companies are Losing Billions to Cyberslackers."

Cover B says, "How an email joke cost Chevron $2.2 million dollars."

The winner?

Cover B outperformed Cover A by more than 24%.

With this valuable knowledge, we were then able to print and mail more "Cover B" magalogs to produce more leads and sales for SurfControl.

246

Harry and David: Shopping Cart Icon Test

Harry and David conducted this test on the shopping cart icon on their website during their busiest season, in December.

They created two versions of their site header, which included a search box and cart icon:

Version A had the word "Keyword" written inside the search field, a magnifying glass search button and a cart icon with the words "Your Cart" next to it.

Version B had the word "Search" above an empty search field, an arrow for its search button and the word "Cart" for the cart icon.

Version A outsold Version B by double digits.

This test shows just how important it is to test small details that you might consider insignificant. Small tweaks can produce major impact.

Version A may have done better because of its more conventional design – people were familiar with the way the search box and cart button looked, and so they used them.

Version B may have been too unorthodox and new.

The lesson from the story: Test everything.

Testing is critical to refining your strategy and gaining valuable leads. Don't skip this critical step. It could make a massive difference in the results of your campaign.

CHAPTER 29

Addressable TV: Revolutionary New Strategy for Cutting Through Clutter and Targeting Your Prospects

Television is a powerful marketing medium for reaching your prospects.

But television has changed.

Over the last several years, cable TV viewing rates have plummeted. Between the years of 2010 and 2018, traditional pay-TV subscribers dropped by more than

10 million households.

In its place, viewers are turning to streaming TV: platforms like Hulu, Roku and Amazon Prime.

Why?

Streaming TV allows viewers to watch what they want, when they want.

Between 40 and 50 million households in America are now watching TV on streaming services, accounting for roughly 128 million individuals.

And that number only continues to rise.

With 75% of all Americans owning two or more streaming devices, that adds up to a significant amount of viewing time.

What does this mean for advertisers?

For one, it means advertising slots on cable TV will drop in price – meaning running still-powerful infomercials is more cost-effective than ever (see Chapter 12).

But streaming TV also poses a powerful new opportunity: addressable TV, or television that allows advertisers to target specific prospects.

Addressable TV vs. Traditional TV Advertising

Traditionally, advertisers have had to "cast a wide net" in order to reach potential buyers on cable TV.

They run a commercial, and hope that their ad will be relevant to viewers.

That means that audiences often end up watching commercials that aren't of any interest to them: Teenagers watching commercials for baby shampoo, or young adults watching ads for blood pressure medication.

The result is wasted time and money, and audiences that are bored and uninterested.

But addressable TV allows marketers to run ads to targeted prospects and audiences only.

That means a few things:

- Two different households might be watching the same program...but will view different ads...
- Advertisers spend their money only on likely buyers....
- And viewers get to exclusively watch ads that are relevant and interesting to them.

It's a win-win for everybody.

Addressable TV: How it Works

Just like you can on Facebook, Google, Amazon and other advertising platforms, addressable TV allows you to target specific prospects or audiences with your ads.

There are two strategies you can use for addressable TV:

a) You can upload a custom list – for example of hot leads, or existing customers – and target them right on their streaming devices.

b) Or, you can create a look-alike audience of prospects that look and behave just like your best prospects – and target them.

The result?

You have the captive attention of an engaged audience...and you're not competing with other ads simultaneously.

Your audience can watch your ad on any one of their streaming devices, including their television screen, phone, tablet, or laptop or desktop computer.

It's powerful.

In fact, right now, I'm testing addressable TV for an investment newsletter client.

And we're getting great results.

Addressable TV: 4 Strategies to Know

Addressable TV could just become one of your most effective channels for your multichannel, integrated marketing campaign.

Imagine: Your prospects see your targeted ads on their Facebook newsfeeds, in their email inboxes, mailboxes... and finally, during a break in their favorite TV show.

But there are a few best practices to know before getting started...

#1: Keep your ad to 30 seconds.

Addressable TV slots are typically 30 seconds long.

So make sure your ads are powerful, get to the point quickly and have a strong call-to-action.

In direct response TV, 60-second commercials do better than 30-second commercials, and 120-second commercials do better than 60-second commercials.

However, the inventory for 60-second ads and above is rare. Therefore, it's best to make sure you rely upon 30-second ad slots. If you're fortunate enough to get longer time slots, that's great.

#2: Use direct response tactics.

As with any marketing asset you create, use direct response copy and art for your ad.

Display the text on screen, and speak directly to the viewer.

For more best practices on creating video, go to Chapter 27.

#3: Addressable TV is especially powerful during election season.

During political elections, traditional ads get pre-empted and bumped on cable TV.

Addressable TV is an effective way to get strong viewership even when your audience is inundated with political ads.

#4: Keep your marketing message and offer the same.

Remember, your addressable TV ads work just like all other marketing assets in your multichannel, integrated marketing campaign.

Keep your messaging and offer the same to maximize response.

Addressable TV has exciting potential to transform your marketing – and to become one of your most valuable channels in your multichannel, integrated marketing campaign.

It's a powerful strategy for capturing the attention

Now What?

My company, CDMG Inc., has pioneered multichannel, integrated marketing, combining advanced targeting strategies with direct mail, email, pre-roll and digital marketing to the same target audience to produce amazing results.

I take a methodical approach to marketing that is different from branding or awareness, targeting prospects with direct response marketing for maximum response … and profits.

These principles have turned small startups into successful, medium-sized businesses … and medium-sized businesses into multimillion-dollar companies.

So, here's what I suggest:

1.   Call Caleb Huey at (615) 490-8823 or email him at caleb@cdmginc.com. Let's start a dialogue, discuss your goals and outline a strategic plan. If you would like, you are welcome to come to our offices in Torrance, California, or Nashville, Tennessee, and see our work, staff and 90 awards my team and I at Creative Direct Marketing Group have won for creating successful, winning campaigns.

But if you can't visit us in person, that's okay. Over 75% of my clients have never been to our office.

2.   I can then send you a very tight proposal on the project: costs, strategy and schedule. The good news: I will reduce your risk and help you succeed in raising capital.

I look forward to talking with you. Answering your questions. Helping you generate new capital. Creative Direct Marketing Group is here to help. So, give us a call at (615) 814-6633 or email Caleb at caleb@cdmginc.com.

Order Your Copy of

The New Multichannel, Integrated Marketing: 29 Trends for Creating a Multichannel, Integrated Campaign to Boost Your Profits Now

First-Time Buyers Receive 20% Off
Order More Than One Book and Receive 30% Off

2 WAYS TO ORDER

Order by phone at (310) 212-5727

Send this form to:
Creative Direct Marketing Group, Inc.
Attn: Craig Huey
21171 S. Western Ave., Suite 260
Torrance, CA 90501

✓ Yes! I want to learn how to effectively raise capital under the JOBS Act for my growing business. Please send me my discounted copy of *The New Multichannel, Integrated Marketing: 29 Trends for Creating a Multichannel, Integrated Campaign to Boost Your Profits Now*

TWO PURCHASING OPTIONS (CHECK ONE):

☐ **Save 20%.** Get 1 copy of *The New Multichannel, Integrated Marketing: 29 Trends for Creating a Multichannel, Integrated Campaign to Boost Your Profits Now*– valued at $24.95 – for only **$19.95**

OR

☐ **Save Up to 30%.** Send me _____ copies of *Multichannel Integrated Marketing: 28 New Insider Secrets for Scientifically Proven Explosive Response, Market Domination and Supercharging Profits* for only **$16.95** per copy

METHOD OF PAYMENT:

_____Check or money order made out to **Creative Direct Marketing Agency**

Charge my: _____VISA _____MasterCard _____American Express

Name (as it appears on card) _____

Card Number _____

Exp Date _____ 3-4 Digit Security Code_____

Signature _____

Street Address _____

City, State, ZIP _____

Email _____Phone #_____

✓ Please sign me up for ***Direct Marketing Update*** – Craig's weekly marketing newsletter on the latest advertising and marketing breakthroughs, plus concise tactics, case studies, test results and tips all delivered directly to my inbox.

MAIL THIS FORM TO:

Creative Direct Marketing Group, Inc., Attn: Craig Huey
21171 S. Western Ave., Suite 260, Torrance, CA 90501
Or, visit **www.multichannelintegratedmarketingbook.com** to purchase a copy online today.

Made in the USA
Columbia, SC
09 February 2023

11621386R00146